AF479124

JESUS
The Story of His Life

Walter Barnett

JESUS
The Story of His Life

A Modern Retelling
Based on the Gospels

Nelson-Hall nh Chicago

Library of Congress Cataloging in Publication Data
Barnett, Walter, 1933-
    Jesus, the story of His life.

    Includes index.
    1. Jesus Christ—Biography.   I.   Title.
BT301.2.B28   232.9'01 [B]   75-28260
ISBN 0-88229-308-7

To my mother

Contents

Preface

The objective of this book is to tell the story of Jesus as simply, directly, and forcefully as possible. The only reliable documentation about him is contained in the New Testament. Virtually nothing is known about him from any other source. Yet the New Testament gives not one, but four narratives of his life—the Gospels of Matthew, Mark, Luke, and John—plus a few other bits of information. The four are not only redundant but often seemingly impossible to reconcile. This book takes all the information in the New Testament sources about the events of Jesus' life and weaves them into a single narrative without additional fictional embellishments.

The idea is not new. Similar efforts have been made throughout the centuries, beginning with Tatian's *Diatessaron* composed about 170 A.D. The purpose of this book, however, unlike many of the others, is not to displace or supersede the four gospels nor to force them into "harmony" with each other but to supplement them with a composite portrait of Jesus drawn from all four. It may therefore be useful to those who want to know what Jesus is reported to have said and done but do not wish to read through all four gospels consecutively. Even those who have read and studied all four may find that a combined narrative such as this adds to their understanding and appreciation of the whole.

For those who may be interested in how the book was put together a note on its composition is included at the end. Also included is a brief note on the historical setting for anybody who may be unfamiliar with the background of these events.

I

A Child Is Born

The Birth of John the Baptist Announced to Zechariah

In the time when Herod was King of Judea, there was a priest named Zechariah in Abijah's division of the priesthood. His wife Elizabeth also came from a family of priests. They both lived good lives in God's sight, in full obedience to all the Lord's commandments. But they were childless, because Elizabeth could not get pregnant, and both were now getting well on in years.

Once while Zechariah was serving as a priest before God during his division's tour of duty, he was chosen by lot, in accordance with their custom, to go into the Lord's sanctuary to burn incense. The whole congregation were waiting outside in prayer at this time of the incense offering.

Suddenly one of the Lord's angels appeared to him, standing at the right of the incense altar. Zechariah was startled at the sight and overcome with fear, but the angel reassured him.

"Don't be afraid, Zechariah. God has heard your prayer, and your wife Elizabeth will bear you a son. You are to name him John. You won't be the only one full of joy on this account. Many people will be glad he was born, because he will be a great man in God's sight. He will never touch wine or strong drink. From his very birth he will be filled with the Holy Spirit, and will bring many of the people of Israel back to the Lord their God. He will go in advance as God's herald, full of the spirit and power of the prophet Elijah, to reconcile father and child, to convert rebellion into the wisdom of obedience, and to prepare a people fit for the Lord."

"How can I be sure of this? I'm an old man, and my wife is getting well on in years."

"I am Gabriel. I stand in attendance on God, and I was sent to speak to you and bring you this good news. But you haven't believed my message, which will come true at the proper time. So listen! Because you disbelieved, you will lose your power of speech, and silent you shall remain until the day these things happen."

In the meantime the people were waiting for Zechariah, surprised that he should stay so long in the Temple. When he did come out he was unable to speak to them, and they realized he had seen a vision in the sanctuary. He stood there speechless, gesturing to them.

When his period of service was over, Zechariah returned home. Some time later his wife Elizabeth became pregnant and for five months did not leave the house. "This is the Lord's doing," she thought. "At last he has looked down on me, to remove my public disgrace!"

Jesus' Birth Announced to Mary

In the sixth month of Elizabeth's pregnancy God sent the angel Gabriel to a town in Galilee called Nazareth, with a message for a girl engaged to marry a man by the name of Joseph, who was a descendant of King David. The girl's name was Mary.

The angel came up and said to her, "Greetings! The Lord is with you and bestows his favor on you." But she was deeply disturbed at the words and wondered what kind of greeting this could be. The angel reassured her.

"Don't be afraid, Mary. God has been gracious to you. You will become pregnant and give birth to a son. You are to name him Jesus. He will be great and will be called 'Son of the Highest.' The Lord God will give him the throne of his ancestor David, and he will be king over the House of Jacob forever. His reign will never end."

"How can this be, considering I don't have a husband?"

"The Holy Spirit will come down on you, and the power of the Highest will overshadow you, and that's why the holy child to be born will be called 'Son of God.' Remember your relative Elizabeth? Well, she who was said to be barren is now six months pregnant in her old age. She is going to have a son too. There is nothing God promises that he can't do."

"Here I am—the Lord's servant. As you have spoken, so be it."

Then the angel left her. Mary got up and hurried off to a town in the hill country of Judah. She went into Zechariah's house and greeted Elizabeth. When Elizabeth heard Mary's greeting, the baby stirred within her. Elizabeth was filled with the Holy Spirit and cried out loud.

"God has blessed you among women!—And blessed the child you will bear! Who am I that the mother of my Lord should come visit me? Look! As soon as I heard your greeting, the baby within me jumped for joy. How happy the woman who believed the Lord's promise would come true!

"Sing, my soul, the greatness of the Lord!
Rejoice, my spirit, in God my savior!
Because he has looked down on his lowly
    servant,
And from this day on all generations will
    count me blessed.
So wonderfully has he dealt with me, the
    Almighty,
And holy is his name!
His mercy is sure towards those who fear
    him,
From generation to generation.
He has stretched out his mighty arm,
And put to rout the proud with their
    pretensions.
Emperors he has tumbled from their
    thrones,
But the humble he has lifted high.
The hungry he has filled with good things,
And the rich sent away empty-handed.
He has come to the aid of his servant Israel.
He has kept the promise made to our
    ancestors,

And remembered to show mercy to
    Abraham
And his children's children forever."
Mary stayed with Elizabeth about three months and
then returned home.

The Birth of John the Baptist

The time came for Elizabeth to have her baby, and
she gave birth to a son. When her neighbors and relatives heard how good the Lord had been to her, they all
rejoiced with her.

On the eighth day they came to circumcise the
child, and they were about to name him Zechariah after
his father. But his mother intervened. "No! He is to be
called John."

"But," they objected, "there is nobody in your
family by that name." They gestured to his father, asking what he would like the boy to be called.

Zechariah requested a writing tablet and, to the
astonishment of all, wrote down, "His name is John."
Immediately he was able to speak again, and he started
praising God.

The neighbors were all struck with awe, and the
whole story spread throughout the hill country of
Judea. Everyone who heard it was impressed and wondered, "What will this child become?" because plainly
the Lord's power was with him.

Zechariah his father was filled with the Holy Spirit
and prophesied.

    "Praise be to the Lord, the God of Israel!
    He has come to his people and set them
        free.
    He has raised up for us a mighty savior,

One descended from his servant David.
So he promised. Age after age he proclaimed
    by the lips of his holy prophets,
That he would save us from our enemies,
And from the power of all who hate us,
That he would deal mercifully with our fathers,
And remember his sacred covenant.
Thus he swore to our father Abraham,
To rescue us from enemy hands,
And allow us to serve him without fear,
Holy and righteous before him,
All the days of our life.
You, my child, will be called Prophet of the Highest.
You will be the Lord's herald,
To prepare his road for him,
To give knowledge of salvation to his people,
By the forgiveness of their sins.
In the tender mercy of our God,
Heaven's bright morning will dawn on us,
And shine down on those in darkness, in death's shadow,
Guiding our steps into the paths of peace."

As the child grew up he developed strong in spirit, and he lived out in the wilds until the day he appeared publicly before Israel.

Jesus' Birth Announced to Joseph

This is how the Messiah's birth occurred. Mary his mother was engaged to Joseph, but before they started living together she was found to be pregnant by the

Holy Spirit. Joseph her husband, being a man of principle but not wanting to disgrace her publicly, resolved to divorce her quietly. While he was considering this, one of the Lord's angels appeared to him in a dream.

"Joseph son of David, don't be afraid to take Mary as your wife. It is by the Holy Spirit she has conceived this child. She will give birth to a son, and you are to name him Jesus, because he will save his people from their sins."

All this happened to bring about what the Lord declared through the prophet: "The virgin will become pregnant and give birth to a son, and he will be called *Emmanuel*" (which means "God is with us").

When Joseph woke up he did as the Lord's angel told him, and took Mary as his wife, but he had no intercourse with her until her son was born.

The Birth of Jesus

At that time a decree was issued by the Emperor Augustus for the taking of a census of the whole Roman world. This was the first census, carried out while Quirinius was governing Syria.

Everyone went to his own home town to register. Joseph went from the town of Nazareth in Galilee to Judea, to be registered at the town of David, called Bethlehem, because he was a descendant of David. Mary his spouse went with him to register. She was pregnant, and while they were there the time came for her to have the baby. She gave birth to a son, her first child, wrapped him up snugly, and laid him in a manger because there was no room for them in the inn.

In that same district some shepherds were out in the fields, keeping watch over their flock at night. Suddenly one of the Lord's angels stood in front of them and the Lord's glory shined around them, and they were terrified. The angel reassured them.

"Don't be afraid. Look, I've got good news for you. Great joy is in store for the whole people. This very night in David's town your savior is born—the Lord Messiah! And this is how you will recognize him. You will find a baby all wrapped up, lying in a manger."

All at once a throng of heaven's army joined the angel, singing the praises of God. "Glory to God in the highest! And on earth peace to people who bear his good will!"

When the angels had left them and returned to heaven the shepherds said to each other, "Come on, let's go over to Bethlehem and see this happening the Lord has told us about." So they hurried off and found their way to Mary and Joseph, and the baby lying in the manger.

When they saw him they related what had been told them about this child. All those who heard it were filled with wonder at what the shepherds said. Mary treasured all these things in her memory, pondering over them.

Meanwhile the shepherds returned, glorifying and praising God for everything they had heard and seen. It had been just as the angel had told them.

Visitors From the East

When Jesus was born at Bethlehem in Judea during Herod's reign, astrologers from the East arrived in Jerusalem, asking, "Where is the child born to be King of the Jews? We've seen his star rising in the east and have come to pay homage to him."

King Herod was greatly disturbed when he heard this, and all Jerusalem with him. Assembling all the chief priests and lawyers of the people, he asked them, "Where is it that the Messiah is to be born?"

"At Bethlehem in Judea," they replied. "This is what the prophet wrote.

> 'You, Bethlehem, in the land of Judah,
> Are by no means least among the rulers of
>   Judah.
> Out of you shall come a leader
> To shepherd my people Israel.' "

Then Herod summoned the astrologers to meet him in private and found out from them exactly when the star had appeared. And he sent them on to Bethlehem with these instructions. "Go make a careful search for the child, and when you find him let me know so I can come myself and pay him homage."

They set out at the king's bidding, and the same star they had seen in the east went ahead of them until it stopped over the place where the child lay. At the sight of the star they were overjoyed. Entering the house, they saw the child with Mary his mother and fell on their knees in homage. Then they opened their treasures and offered him gifts—gold, frankincense, and myrrh. And being warned in a dream not to return to Herod, they went back to their own land by another road.

Jesus Circumcised and Presented to God

When the baby was a week old it was time to circumcise him, and Joseph named him Jesus—the name given by the angel before he was conceived.

Then, after their purification had been completed according to the Law of Moses, they brought him up to Jerusalem to present him to the Lord. (This is what the

Lord's law prescribes. "Every first-born male shall be dedicated to the Lord.") And they also came to offer a sacrifice as required by the law of the Lord—"a pair of turtle doves, or two young pigeons."

In Jerusalem at the time there was a man by the name of Simeon. He was upright and devout, one who watched and waited for the consolation of Israel, and the Holy Spirit was on him. He had been assured by the Holy Spirit that he would not die until he had seen the Lord's Messiah.

Led by the Spirit, Simeon came into the Temple. When the parents brought in the child Jesus to do for him what the Law made customary, he took the child in his arms and gave thanks to God.

"Now, Lord, you have kept your promise.
Let your servant go in peace.
With my own eyes I have seen your
    salvation,
Which you have prepared in the presence of
    all nations,
A light to reveal your way to the Gentiles,
And to give glory to your people Israel."

The child's father and mother were full of wonder at the things Simeon said about him. Simeon blessed them and said to Mary his mother, "Look, this child is destined for a controversial sign to lay bare the secret disposition of many hearts. And many people in Israel will fall and rise because of him. You too will be pierced to the heart."

A prophetess was there as well—Anna the daughter of Phanuel, of the tribe of Asher. She was a very old woman. Following seven years of marriage she had lived as a widow to the age of eighty-four. She never left the Temple but worshipped God day and night, fasting and praying. Coming up at that very moment, she gave thanks to God and spoke about the child to all those who were looking for God to redeem Jerusalem. And Jesus' parents performed everything the Lord's law required.

King Herod's Fury and the Escape to Egypt

One of the Lord's angels appeared to Joseph in a dream. "Get up, take the child and his mother, and escape to Egypt, and stay there till I tell you, because Herod is going to be looking for the child, to do away with him."

So Joseph got up, took mother and child, and left in the night for Egypt, and he stayed there until Herod's death. This happened to carry out what the Lord had declared through the prophet: "I called my son out of Egypt."

When Herod realized the astrologers had tricked him, he flew into a rage and gave orders to massacre all the boys in Bethlehem and its vicinity who were two years old or less, in accordance with the time he had learned from the astrologers. Thus the words of the prophet Jeremiah were fulfilled:

"A voice was heard in Rama,
The sound of weeping and wailing.
It was Rachel crying for her children,
And she will not be consoled,
Because they are all gone."

The Return to Nazareth

After Herod had died, one of the Lord's angels appeared to Joseph in a dream, in Egypt. "Get up, take the child and his mother, and go to the land of Israel. Those who threatened the child's life are dead."

So Joseph got up, took mother and child with him, and went to the land of Israel. Hearing, however, that

Archelaus had succeeded his father Herod in Judea, Joseph was afraid to go there. So being warned by a dream, he retired to the province of Galilee. On their return to Galilee they settled in their own town, Nazareth. And thus came true the words of the prophets—"He will be called a Nazarene."

The child grew big and strong and full of wisdom, and God's favor was on him.

Jesus at the Age of Twelve

Every year Jesus' parents went to Jerusalem for the Passover festival, and when he was twelve they made the pilgrimage as usual. When the festival was over and they started for home, the boy Jesus stayed behind in Jerusalem. His parents were unaware of this. Supposing him to be in the caravan, they journeyed on for a whole day, and only then did they start looking for him among their friends and relations. Not finding him, they turned back to Jerusalem to hunt for him.

After three days they found him, to their astonishment, in the Temple, sitting surrounded by the teachers, listening to them and putting questions. All those who heard him were amazed at his intelligence and the answers he gave.

"Son," his mother said to him, "why did you do this to us? Look, your father and I have been worried sick, trying to find you."

"Why did you have to hunt for me?" he replied. "Didn't you realize I was bound to be in my Father's house?" But they failed to comprehend his meaning.

He went back with them to Nazareth and was obedient to them, and his mother treasured all these things in her memory. As Jesus grew up, he advanced in wisdom and in favor with God and with people.

II

John the Baptist

A Voice Crying in the Wilderness

In the fifteenth year of the reign of the Emperor Tiberius, when Pontius Pilate was governor of Judea, when Herod Antipas was prince of Galilee, his brother Philip prince of Iturea and Trachonitis, and Lysanias prince of Abilene, during the high-priesthood of Annas and Caiaphas, the word of God came to John son of Zechariah in the desert. And he went all over the Jordan River region, preaching in the Judean desert, calling on the people, "Repent! Turn from your sins and be baptized, and God will forgive you. The kingdom of heaven is at hand!" Just as the prophet Isaiah had written:

"Here is my herald.

I will send him on ahead of you,

To open up the way."
"A voice crying in the wilderness,
'Prepare a road for the Lord!
Clear a straight path for him!
Every valley must be filled in,
And every hill and mountain leveled.
The crooked turns must be straightened
    out,
The rough places smoothed over,
And all humanity will see God's salvation!' "
John was dressed in a rough coat of camel's hair with a leather belt around his waist, and his food was locusts and wild honey. The people flocked to him from Jerusalem and all parts of Judea and the Jordan River region and were baptized by him in the Jordan, confessing their sins.

But when he saw many of the Pharisees and Sadducees coming for baptism, he said to them, "You snakes! Who warned you to run from the wrath to come? Bear fruits that befit repentance, and don't presume to tell yourselves, 'We are descendants of Abraham.' I tell you, God could take these rocks and make children for Abraham! The ax is already slashing at the roots of the trees. Every tree that fails to produce good fruit is cut down and thrown on the fire."

The crowds asked him, "Then what are we to do?"

"Whoever has two shirts must share with the one who has none, and whoever has food must do likewise."

Among those who came to be baptized were some tax collectors, and they asked him, "Teacher, what are we to do?"

"Don't collect more than the assessment."

Soldiers also came, asking, "And we, what about us?"

"No bullying! No blackmail! Be content with your pay."

The people were all full of expectation, wondering about John. Could he be the promised Messiah? But he said, "I baptize you with water to show your repentance, but one is coming after me who is much greater than I am, whose sandals I am unworthy to stoop down and untie or even to carry. He will baptize you with the Holy Spirit and with fire. He has his winnowing fork in hand, to clear his threshing floor and to gather the wheat into his barn, but the chaff he will burn with unquenchable fire." Thus with many other challenging words he proclaimed the good news to the people.

Jesus Baptized by John

At the same time Jesus came to the Jordan from Nazareth in Galilee, to be baptized by John. John tried to dissuade him.

"Do you come to me? Instead, I ought to be baptized by you."

But Jesus replied, "Let it be this way for now, because we thus appropriately carry out everything God requires." So John agreed.

Jesus was baptized by John in the Jordan, and as soon as he came up out of the water, praying, he saw the heavens torn open and the Spirit of God coming down like a dove to settle on him. And a voice came from heaven, "You are my own dear son. I am delighted with you!"

When Jesus thus began his work, he was about thirty years old.

The Testing of Jesus

Jesus came away from the Jordan filled with the Holy Spirit, and the Spirit immediately drove him into the desert, among the wild animals, where he stayed for a long time, tested by the devil. During all this time he was fasting, and as it drew to a close he was ravenous with hunger.

The devil suggested to him, "If you are the Son of God, order these stones to turn into bread."

But Jesus answered, "Scripture says, 'Man cannot live on bread alone, but on every word God speaks.'"

Then the devil whisked him to Jerusalem, the Holy City, to the pinnacle of the Temple and suggested, "If you are the Son of God, throw yourself down from here, because scripture says, 'He will give his angels charge of you, to guard you,' and 'They will bear you up in their arms, so you won't even hurt your feet on the stones.'"

Jesus replied, "But scripture also says, 'You are not to test the Lord your God.'"

Again, from a towering mountain the devil showed him in a flash all the world's kingdoms in their greatness and suggested to him, "I will give you all this power and glory. It has been handed over to me, and I give it to anyone I please. So if you will kneel down and worship me, it will all be yours."

"Get away, Satan!" Jesus cried. "The scripture says, 'You shall worship the Lord your God and serve him alone.'"

So when the devil had finished all his temptations he left him for the time being, and angels came to Jesus' aid.

John Points to Jesus

This is the testimony John gave when the Pharisees sent priests and Levites from Jerusalem to ask him who he was. John did not refuse to answer but confessed plainly that he was not the Messiah.

"What then?" they asked him. "Are you Elijah?"

"I am not."

"Are you the prophet?"

"No."

"Then tell us who you are. We have to take an answer back to those who sent us. What do you say about yourself?"

"This is what I am. 'The voice of one crying in the wilderness, "Make straight the highway of the Lord",' in the words of the prophet Isaiah."

"Then why are you baptizing, if you're neither the Messiah, nor Elijah, nor the prophet?"

"I baptize with water, but among you stands one you don't know, the one who is coming after me, the thong of whose sandal I am not fit to untie."

This took place at Bethany on the other side of the Jordan, where John was baptizing.

The next day John saw Jesus coming towards him.

"Look!" he said, "The Lamb of God, who takes away the sin of the world! This is the one of whom I said, 'After me comes a man who ranks before me,' because he existed before I was born. Even I didn't know who it would be, but for this very purpose I came baptizing with water—to reveal him to Israel."

This was John's testimony. "I saw the Spirit come down from heaven like a dove and rest on him. I myself didn't know who it would be, but the one who sent me to baptize with water told me, 'The man on whom you see the Spirit come down and stay is the one who is to baptize with the Holy Spirit.' I have seen it and given my witness that this is God's Chosen One."

Jesus' First Disciples

The following day John was standing there again with two of his disciples when Jesus passed by. Looking at him, John said, "There goes the Lamb of God!" The two disciples heard him say this and followed Jesus. Jesus turned and saw them following.

"What do you want?" he asked.

"Rabbi " (which means "Teacher"), "where are you staying?"

"Come and see."

So they came and saw where he was staying, and they spent the rest of the day with him because it was about four o'clock in the afternoon.

One of the two who heard John speak and followed Jesus was Andrew, Simon Peter's brother. The first thing he did was to find his brother Simon and tell him, "We have found the Messiah!" (which is the same as "Christ" and means the "anointed one"). And he brought him to Jesus.

Jesus looked him over. "So you're Simon son of John. You will be called Cephas" (which is the same as "Peter" and means "rock").

The next day Jesus decided to go to Galilee. He found Philip, who like Andrew and Peter came from Bethsaida, and said to him, "Follow me."

Philip went to find Nathanael and told him, "We have met the man spoken of by Moses in the Law and by the prophets too—Jesus son of Joseph, from Nazareth."

"Nazareth!" exclaimed Nathanael. "Can anything good come out of Nazareth?"

"Come and see."

When Jesus saw Nathanael approaching, he said of him, "Here is an Israelite worthy of the name. There is nothing false in him."

"How do you know me?" Nathanael asked.

"I saw you when you were under the fig tree, before **Philip called you.**"

"Rabbi," exclaimed Nathanael, "You are the Son of God! You are the King of Israel!"

"Do you believe just because I told you I saw you under the fig tree? You will see greater things than this." Then Jesus added, "I am telling you the truth, you will see heaven wide open and God's angels going up and coming down by way of the Son of Man."

Water Into Wine

On the third day there was a wedding at Cana in Galilee to which Jesus and his disciples were invited. His mother was there too.

When the wine gave out, Jesus' mother said to him, "They've run out of wine."

"You must not tell me what to do, woman," he replied. "My time has not yet come."

His mother told the servants, "Do whatever he tells you."

Six stone jars were standing there for the Jewish rites of purification, each capable of holding twenty or thirty gallons. Jesus told the servants to fill the jars with water, and they filled them up to the brim.

"Now draw some out," he said, "and take it to the person in charge of arrangements for the feast." And they did so.

When this person tasted the water now become wine, not knowing where it came from (though the servants who had drawn the water knew), he called the bridegroom and told him, "Everyone serves the best wine first and then, when the guests have had plenty to drink, the ordinary wine. But you have kept the best until now!"

This deed at Cana in Galilee was the first of the

signs by which Jesus revealed his glory and led his disciples to believe in him. Afterwards, he went down to Capernaum in company with his mother, his brothers, and his disciples, and they stayed there a few days.

The Interview With Nicodemus

As it was near the time of the Jewish Passover, Jesus went up to Jerusalem. While he was there during the festival, many people gave him their allegiance when they saw the signs he performed. But Jesus did not entrust himself to them because he knew people, all of them. He needed no testimony from anybody about a person because he knew himself what was inside the person.

One of the Jewish leaders—a Pharisee named Nicodemus—came at night to talk with him.

"Rabbi, we know you are a teacher from God. Nobody could do these great things you are doing, unless God were with him."

"I'm telling you the truth," Jesus replied, "unless a person is born all over again, he cannot see the kingdom of God."

"How can a grown man be born again? Can he get back inside his mother and be born a second time?"

"I'm telling you the truth. Unless one is born of water and the Spirit, he cannot enter the kingdom of God. What is born of the flesh is flesh. The Spirit alone gives birth to spirit. So you shouldn't be surprised that I told you, 'You must be born again.' The wind blows wherever it pleases, and you hear the sound of it, but you don't know where it comes from or where it's going. So it is with everyone born of the Spirit."

"How can this be?" queried Nicodemus.

"What!" said Jesus, "You the teacher of Israel, and

you don't understand this? I'm telling you the truth. We speak of what we know and testify to what we've seen, yet you all reject our testimony. If you don't believe me when I talk to you about things on earth, how will you ever believe me if I should tell you about the things of heaven?

"No one ever went up into heaven except the one who came down from heaven—the Son of Man. And just as Moses lifted up the bronze snake on a pole in the desert, the Son of Man must be lifted up, so that whoever believes in him may possess eternal life.

"God loved the world so much he gave his only son, in order that everyone who believes in him may not die but have eternal life. God did not send the Son into the world to be its judge, but to be its savior.

"Whoever believes in him does not come under judgment, but the unbeliever has already been judged in that he has refused his allegiance to God's only son. This is the test. The light has come into the world, but people preferred darkness to light because their deeds were evil. Everyone who does wrong hates the light and avoids it, to keep his deeds from exposure. But the honest person comes to the light so it can be clearly seen that God is in everything he does."

John Passes the Torch to Jesus

After this, Jesus and his disciples went into the Judean countryside, where he spent some time with them and baptized. John too was baptizing at Aenon near Salim, because there was plenty of water there. And people came and were baptized. (John had not yet been imprisoned.)

A dispute over purification arose between John's disciples and a Jew. They came to John and told him,

"Rabbi, that man who was with you on the other side of the Jordan, about whom you testified, is here baptizing, and everybody is flocking to him."

"One can have only what God gives him," John answered. "You yourselves bear me witness that I said, 'I am not the Messiah, but I have been sent on ahead of him.' The bride belongs to the bridegroom. The bridegroom's best man, who stands by and listens for him, is overjoyed when he hears the groom's voice. That joy is now mine and it is complete. As he grows in importance, I must diminish."

John Imprisoned by Herod Antipas

Herod the prince had John arrested and locked up in prison at Macherus, giving as a reason his fear that the great influence John exercised over the people might make it possible for John to raise a rebellion. John had severely criticized Herod for all his evil deeds and for taking as his wife Herodias, who had been married to his brother.

When Jesus learned of this and that the Pharisees had heard he was making and baptizing more disciples than John (though it was not Jesus who baptized, but rather his disciples), he left Judea and set out once more for Galilee, but he had to pass through Samaria on the way.

The Samaritan Woman

Jesus came to the Samaritan town of Sychar, near the field Jacob gave his son Joseph, and stopped at Jacob's well there, tired by the trip, while his disciples went into the town to buy food. It was about noon, and a Samaritan woman came to the well to draw water. Jesus asked her for a drink.

"What! You, a Jew, ask a drink from me, a Samaritan woman?" (Jews refuse to drink from the same cup with Samaritans.)

"If you only knew what God gives and who it is that's asking you for a drink, you would have asked him, and he would have given you living water."

"Sir, you don't have any bucket and this well is deep. How can you give me 'living water'? Are you greater than our ancestor Jacob who gave us this well and drank from it himself, he and his sons and his cattle too?"

"Everyone who drinks this water will get thirsty again, but whoever drinks the water I give him will never be thirsty. The water I give him will become in him a spring welling up into eternal life."

"Sir, give me this water of yours, so I won't be thirsty or have to come all this way to get some."

"Go call your husband and come here."

"I don't have a husband."

"You are right in saying you don't have a husband. Although you have been married five times, the man you're living with now is not your husband. In this you spoke the truth."

"Sir, I can see you are a prophet. Our Samaritan ancestors worshipped God on this mountain, but you Jews say the place where people ought to worship is in Jerusalem."

"Woman, believe me, the time is coming when you will worship the Father neither on this mountain nor in Jerusalem. You Samaritans worship without knowing what you worship, while we worship what we know, because salvation comes from the Jews. But the time is approaching, indeed it is already here, when the real worshippers will worship the Father in spirit and in truth. These are the kind of worshippers the Father seeks. God is spirit, and those who worship him must worship in spirit and in truth."

"I know the Messiah—the one called "anointed"— is coming. When he comes, he will tell us everything."

"I who speak to you am he."

Just then Jesus' disciples returned and were surprised to find him talking with a woman, but none of them asked him what he wanted or why he was talking with her. As for the woman, she left her waterpot and went back to town to spread the word, "Come see a man who told me everything I ever did. Could this be the Messiah?"

The people came out of the town and were on their way to him. Meanwhile the disciples begged him to eat.

"I have food you know nothing about," he told them.

At this the disciples turned to each other. "Could someone have brought him food?"

Jesus responded, "My food is to do the will of the one who sent me and to complete his work. You say, 'Four months more and then comes the harvest.' I tell you, look up and see how the fields are already white, ripe for harvest. The harvester draws pay and gathers crops for eternal life so that sower and harvester can celebrate together, because here the saying holds true, 'One sows and another harvests.' I have sent you to harvest a crop for which you never toiled. Others worked, and you have come in to gather the fruits of their labors."

When the Samaritans arrived from the town they asked him to stay with them, and he stayed there two days. Many of them had believed in him because of the woman's testimony, but many more came to believe because of what they heard from his own lips. They told the woman, "We believe now, not because of what you said, but because we have heard for ourselves, and we know he really is the savior of the world."

III

The "Galilean Springtime"

Jesus Arrives in Galilee

When Jesus arrived in Galilee full of the power of the Spirit the Galileans welcomed him. They too had gone to the festival and seen everything he had done in Jerusalem at Passover. Reports about him spread throughout the countryside. He began to preach God's good news and to teach in their synagogues.

"The time has come. The kingdom of God is at hand. Repent and believe in the good news."

And everybody praised him.

The Official's Boy

Once again he visited Cana in Galilee where he had turned the water into wine. At another town, Capernaum, the son of an official lay ill. When the official heard that Jesus had come from Judea to Galilee he went and begged Jesus to go down and heal his son, who was at the point of death.

Jesus said to him, "Will none of you ever believe without seeing signs and wonders?"

"Sir," the official pleaded, "come down before my boy dies."

"Go on home. Your son will live."

The man believed Jesus and went his way. As he was returning to Capernaum, his servants met him with the news, "Your boy is going to live!" So he asked them when his son began to improve.

"Yesterday at one in the afternoon the fever left him."

The father remembered that this was the time Jesus had told him, "Your son will live," and he himself believed, and his entire household as well.

This now was the second sign Jesus performed in Galilee.

Nazareth Rejects Jesus

Jesus went to Nazareth where he had been brought up, and on the Sabbath day he went as usual to the synagogue. He stood up to read the lesson and was handed the scroll of the prophet Isaiah. He opened the scroll and found the place where it was written:

> "The Spirit of the Lord is on me because he
>   has anointed me.
> He has sent me to announce good news to
>   the poor,
> To proclaim release for the captives and
>   recovery of sight for the blind,
> To set free the oppressed,
> To proclaim the year of the Lord's favor."

Jesus rolled up the scroll, gave it back to the attendant, and sat down. The eyes of everyone in the synagogue were fixed on him. He began to speak.

"Today in your very hearing this text has come true."

Surprised that words of such grace should come from his lips, they were all impressed and asked each other, "Isn't this Joseph's son?"

"No doubt," he told them, "you will quote me the proverb, 'Physician, heal yourself!' and say, 'We've heard what you did at Capernaum. Now do the same here in your own home town.' But it is true, I tell you, no prophet is recognized in his own country. There were many widows in Israel, you can be sure, in Elijah's day, when for three years and six months there was no rain and famine spread over the whole land. Yet Elijah was not sent to any of them. He was sent only to a widow at Sarepta in the territory of Sidon. And there were many lepers in Israel at the time of the prophet Elisha, and not one of them was healed, but only Naaman the Syrian."

At these words the entire congregation became infuriated. They jumped up and threw Jesus out of the town, taking him to the edge of the hill on which it was built, to hurl him headlong off the cliff. But he walked right through them and went away.

Jesus Calls Four Fishermen to Follow Him

So Jesus left Nazareth and went down and lived in Capernaum by the Sea of Galilee, in the country of Zebulun and Naphtali, thus fulfilling Isaiah's prophecy:
"Land of Zebulun and land of Naphtali,
On the way to the sea, across the Jordan,

Galilee of the Gentiles!
The people sitting in darkness have seen
    a great light.
For those in the land and shadow of death
    light has dawned."

While he was standing on the lakeshore and the people were pressing in on him to hear the word of God, he saw two boats pulled up on the beach. The fishermen had come ashore and were washing and mending their nets. One of the boats belonged to Simon Peter. He and his brother Andrew happened to be fishermen. Getting into the boat, Jesus asked Simon to put out a little from the shore, and he sat down and taught the people from the boat.

When he had finished speaking he said to Simon, "Now put out into the deep water and let down your nets for a catch."

"Master, we worked all night and caught nothing. But if you say so I'll let down the nets."

They did so and enclosed a great shoal of fish. As their nets were breaking, they beckoned to their partners in the other boat to come and help them. They came and filled both boats almost to the point of sinking. When Simon Peter saw what had happened he fell down at Jesus' knees.

"Leave me, Lord," he begged, "I'm a sinner!" He and his companions were all astonished at the catch of fish they had taken, and so were his partners James and John the sons of Zebedee.

"Don't be afraid," Jesus told them. "Follow me and I'll teach you how to catch people."

When they brought their boats to land they abandoned everything and followed him, leaving Zebedee and the hired men behind in the boat.

"Even the Demons Obey Him"

They went into Capernaum, and on the Sabbath Jesus entered the synagogue and began to teach. The people who heard him were astounded at his teaching because, unlike the lawyers, he taught with a note of authority.

Now a man possessed by an unclean spirit happened to be in the synagogue at the time and screamed, "What do you want with us, Jesus of Nazareth? Have you come to destroy us? I know who you are. You're God's Holy One!"

Jesus rebuked the spirit. "Be quiet! Come out of him!"

The demon threw the man down in front of them all, racking him with convulsions, and, giving a loud scream, came out without harming him. The people were all amazed and full of questions.

"What's this? Some new kind of teaching? This man speaks with power and authority, and when he gives orders even the unclean spirits obey him!"

His fame spread quickly throughout all the surrounding region of Galilee.

Peter's Mother-in-Law

Jesus got up and left the synagogue and went straight to the house of Simon and Andrew. James and John accompanied them.

Simon's mother-in-law was sick in bed with a high fever, and they told him about her immediately. Jesus came and stood over her and rebuked the fever, and it left her. He took her by the hand and helped her to her feet, and she waited on them.

That evening at sundown people brought him their sick and those possessed by demons, and the whole town crowded around the door. Jesus laid his hands on the sick and healed them and cast out the spirits with a word. As the demons came out of those possessed they shouted, "You are the Son of God!" But he cut them short and refused to allow them to speak, because they knew he was the Messiah. So Isaiah's prophecy came true: "He took our illnesses and carried away our diseases."

In the morning a long time before daybreak Jesus got up and went out to a deserted spot and prayed. Simon and his companions followed Jesus and when they found him told him, "Everyone is looking for you."

"Let us go on to the next towns," he replied, "so I can preach there too. That's what I came out to do."

The people went looking for him and came up and tried to keep him from leaving them, but he told them, "I have to proclaim the good news of God's kingdom to the other towns too. This is what I was sent to do."

So Jesus went throughout Galilee, teaching in the synagogues, preaching the good news of the kingdom, healing every disease and infirmity of the people, and driving out the demons. The news of him spread all over Syria, and they brought him all the sick and afflicted, the demon-possessed, the epileptics, and the paralytics, and he healed them. Great crowds trailed him from Galilee and the Ten Towns, from Jerusalem and Judea, and even from the lands across the Jordan River.

Jesus Touches the Untouchable

While Jesus was in one of the towns, a man all covered with leprosy saw him and came up and fell on his knees in front of him, begging him, "Sir, if you want to, you can make me clean."

Moved with pity, Jesus reached out and touched him. "I do want to. Be clean." The leprosy left him immediately, and he was clean.

Jesus sent him off with strict orders. "See to it you say nothing about this to anybody! Go straight to the priest and let him examine you. Then offer the sacrifice for your cleansing that Moses commanded, as a witness to them."

But the man went out and began spreading the news. In fact, he talked so freely that Jesus could no longer enter a town publicly, because of the massive throngs that collected to hear him and have their diseases healed. So he stayed out in the countryside, and people kept coming to him from every quarter. But from time to time he would retire into the wilds and pray.

A Paralytic Lowered Through the Roof

When after some time he returned to Capernaum the news went around that he was home. Such a crowd collected that there was not enough room for them, not even in the space outside the door. And God's healing power was with him.

While Jesus was teaching them, four men came carrying a paralytic. When they could not get near him because of the crowd they climbed up on the roof, made a hole in it, and let the stretcher down on which the sick man was lying, right in front of Jesus.

When Jesus saw their faith he said to the paralyzed man, "Courage, my son! Your sins are forgiven."

Some lawyers and Pharisees were sitting there who had come from the towns of Galilee and Judea and from Jerusalem, and, hearing what Jesus said to the man, they muttered to themselves, "How can he say such a thing? It's blasphemy! Only God can forgive sins."

Jesus, reading their minds, addressed them. "Why do you think such thoughts? Which is easier, to say to this paralyzed man, 'Your sins are forgiven,' or to say, 'Get up, pick up your mat, and walk'? But to show you that the Son of Man has authority on earth to forgive sins," he turned and said to the paralytic, "I tell you, stand up, take your bed, and go home!"

In front of everybody the paralytic got up, picked up his stretcher, and walked out of the house, praising God.

Struck with awe and amazement, the crowds praised God for having given such authority to human beings. "We've never seen anything like this before!"

"I Came to Call the Outcasts"

After this Jesus went back out to the lakeshore. The whole crowd gathered around him, and he taught them. As he went on from there Jesus passed the customs-house and saw a tax collector sitting there by the name of Levi (or Matthew), the son of Alphaeus.

"Follow me," Jesus told him. And Levi got up, left everything, and followed him.

Levi gave a great banquet at his home in honor of Jesus, and to it came many of his fellow tax collectors and other outcasts. (There were many such who followed Jesus.)

While they were together at the table, the Pharisees and the lawyers who belonged to their party complained to Jesus' disciples. "Why do you and your teacher eat and drink with tax collectors and sinners?"

Jesus overheard them and answered, "Healthy people don't need a doctor. The sick do. Go find out what this scripture means: 'I want mercy, not sacrifice.' It's not the virtuous I came to call, but sinners to repentance."

Feasting Instead of Fasting

People asked Jesus, "Why do John's disciples and those of the Pharisees fast and pray so often, but yours eat and drink?"

"Can you make wedding guests be sad and go without food while the bridegroom is with them? As long as they have him with them, they can't do that. But the time will come when the bridegroom is taken away from them, and at that time they will go without food."

"You Cannot Mix Old Ways With New"

He pictured it to them this way. "Nobody patches an old coat with a piece of new cloth. If he does, the patch shrinks, tearing away from it, the new from the old, leaving a bigger hole. Nor would the new piece match the old.

"Nobody puts new wine into used wineskins. If he does, the new wine will burst the skins, and wine and skins are both lost. You need fresh skins for new wine, then both will stay in good shape.

"And no one wants new wine after drinking old wine. 'The old is better,' he says."

A Visit to Jerusalem: The Cripple at the Pool of Bethzatha

Later on, Jesus went up to Jerusalem for one of the Jewish festivals. There near the Sheep Gate is a pool with five porches, the Hebrew name of which is Bethzatha. On these porches throngs of invalids were lying— the blind, the lame, and the paralyzed. One man was there who had been crippled for thirty-eight years. Jesus saw him lying there and realized he had been ill a long time.

"Do you want to be healed?" he asked him.

"Sir, I don't have anyone to put me in the pool when the water is stirred up, and while I'm trying to reach it, somebody else manages to get in before me."

Jesus told him to stand up, pick up his bed, and walk. The man recovered at once, took up his pallet, and began to walk.

Now the day on which this occurred was a Sabbath, so the Jews said to the man who was cured, "This is the Sabbath. You are not allowed to carry your pallet on the Sabbath."

"The man who made me well told me to pick up my pallet and walk."

"Who was it that told you to take up your pallet and walk?" But the man who had been healed did not know who it was, because Jesus had disappeared in the crowd.

Later Jesus found him in the Temple and said to him, "Now that you are well, don't sin any more or something worse may happen to you."

The man went off and told the Jews it was Jesus who had healed him. This is why they persecuted Jesus, because he broke the rules of the Sabbath. His defense to this charge was, "My Father never stops working, so I am working." This made the Jews even more determined to kill him, because he not only broke the Sabbath law but also called God his own father, thus claiming equality with God.

Jesus told them, "I am telling you the truth. The Son cannot do anything on his own. He does only what he sees the Father doing. Whatever the Father does, the Son does. The Father loves the Son and shows him all his works and will show him even greater works than these, to fill you with wonder. Just as the Father raises the dead and gives them life, the Son too gives life to anyone he pleases.

"Again, the Father doesn't judge anyone but has turned full jurisdiction over to the Son. It is his will that everyone should honor the Son just as they honor the Father. To deny honor to the Son is to deny it to the Father who sent him.

"I am telling you the truth. Whoever hears my word and believes the one who sent me has eternal life. He does not come up for judgment but has already passed from death to life. I tell you the time is coming, indeed it is already here, when the dead will hear the voice of the Son of God, and all those who hear will come to life. Just as the Father himself is the source of life, he has made the Son a source of life.

"As Son of Man he has also been given the right to pass judgment. Don't be surprised at this. The time is coming when all those in the grave will hear his voice and come out, those who have done good, to the resurrection of life, and those who have done wrong, to the resurrection of judgment. I cannot act on my own. I judge only as I am instructed. And my judgment is just, because I don't seek to do my own will but only the will of the one who sent me.

"If I testify on my own behalf, such testimony is suspect. There is somebody else who bears witness to me, and I know his testimony is true. Your messengers have been to John. You have his witness to the truth. Not that I rely on human testimony, but I remind you of it for your own salvation. John was like a brightly burning lamp, and for a time you were willing to bask in his light. But I rely on a testimony even greater than

John's. The works the Father gave me to complete, these very works I am doing, are testimony enough that he sent me. Moreover, the Father who sent me, whose voice you have never heard, whose form you have never seen, has borne witness to me himself. And his word finds no welcome in you, because you don't believe the one he has sent. You pore over the scriptures, because you think in them you've got eternal life. Yet, although their testimony points to me, you refuse to come to me for that life.

"I don't look to people for honor. But with you it is different, as I well know. You have no love for God in your hearts. I have come accredited by my Father, and you have no welcome for me, but if somebody else comes self-accredited, you will receive him with open arms. How can you believe, as long as you seek honor from each other and care nothing for the honor that comes from the one and only God?

"Don't imagine I will be your accuser before the Father. It is Moses who will accuse you, the very Moses on whom you set your hope. If you really believed Moses you would believe me, because he wrote about me. But if you don't believe what he wrote, how can you believe what I say?"

The Sabbath Broken Again in the Wheatfields

One Sabbath Jesus was passing through some wheatfields. His disciples were hungry so they began to pick the heads of wheat, rub them in their hands, and eat the grain.

Some of the Pharisees asked him, "Look! Why are they doing what is forbidden on the Sabbath?"

"Haven't you ever read what David did when he and his companions were hungry and in need? He went into the house of God and took and ate the consecrated bread, which only the priests are allowed to eat, and also gave it to his companions. And haven't you read in the Law how on the Sabbath the priests in the Temple actually break the Sabbath and it is not held against them? I tell you, what is here is greater than the Temple.

"And if you had known what this scripture means, 'I want mercy, not sacrifice,' you would not have condemned the innocent. The Sabbath was made for the sake of humanity, not the other way around. So the Son of Man is lord even over the Sabbath."

Another Sabbath Controversy: The Man With the Crippled Hand

On another Sabbath Jesus entered a synagogue and taught. A man was there whose right hand was crippled. The lawyers and the Pharisees were watching to see whether he would heal on the Sabbath so they might accuse him of breaking the law. But he knew their intentions.

"Come stand up here," he told the man with the crippled hand. And the man got up and stood there.

Then Jesus said to them, "What if you had one sheep and it fell in a ditch on the Sabbath? Is there a man among you who would not catch hold of it and lift it out? How much more is a man worth than a sheep! So I ask you, what does our Law allow us to do on the Sabbath? To do good or to do harm, to save life or to destroy it?" But they held their peace.

He looked around at them, with anger and sorrow at their callousness, then he addressed the man. "Stretch out your hand." He stretched it out and it became well again, just like the other.

The Pharisees were filled with rage and went out and discussed with each other what they could do to Jesus. And they immediately began plotting with the Herodians to destroy him.

By the Sea of Galilee

Jesus, aware of this, retired to the lake with his disciples, and a great throng from Galilee followed. Many others, hearing everything he was doing, came from Judea, Jerusalem, and Idumea, from the other side of the Jordan, and from the neighborhood of Tyre and Sidon as well.

He told his disciples to have a boat ready for him to save him from being crushed by the crowd, because he had cured so many people that all the sick kept pressing forward to touch him. And he healed them all.

Those possessed by unclean spirits, whenever they saw him, would fall down in front of him and cry out, "You are the Son of God!" And he gave them strict orders not to make him known.

Thus the words of the prophet Isaiah came true:
"Here is my servant I have chosen,
My beloved in whom my soul delights.
I will put my Spirit upon him,
And he will announce justice to the Gentiles.
He will not quarrel or shout,
Nor will anyone hear his voice in the
    streets.
He will not crush a bruised reed,
Nor put out a smoldering wick.
He will persist till he makes justice
    victorious,
And his name will be the hope of the
    Gentiles."

The Selection of the Twelve

During this period he went out into the hills to pray and spent the whole night in prayer to God. At daybreak he called his disciples and chose twelve of them, whom he called "messengers," to be his companions and to be sent out to preach, with authority to drive out demons.

These were Simon, whom he named Peter, and Andrew, Simon's brother; James and John the sons of Zebedee, whom he named *Boanerges* (which means "thunderbolts"); Philip and Bartholomew; Matthew the tax collector and Thomas; James the son of Alphaeus and Judas, James' son (or Thaddaeus, or Lebbaeus); and Simon the Zealot (or *Cananaean*) and Judas Iscariot the man who betrayed him.

He came down with them to a level place where a great crowd of his disciples had gathered, together with a throng of people from Jerusalem and all Judea and the seacoast of Tyre and Sidon who had come to listen to him and be cured of their diseases. Those who were troubled by unclean spirits were restored to health, and the whole crowd tried to touch him, because power came out of him, healing them all.

The Sermon on the Mount

Jesus, seeing the crowds, went up the hill, and when he had taken his seat his disciples gathered around. Turning his gaze toward them, he began to teach them.

The Beatitudes and the Woes

"Happy are you who are poor and humble!
  The kingdom of God is yours.
Happy are you who now go hungry! You will
  be filled.

Happy are you who are crying and
  mourning! You will be comforted.
  You will laugh.
Happy are you who are gentle in spirit! You
  will possess the earth.
Happy are you who hunger and thirst to see
  right prevail! You will be satisfied.
Happy are you who forgive others! God will
  forgive you.
Happy are you with a pure heart! You will
  see God.
Happy are you who strive to make peace
  among people! God will call
  you his children.
Happy are you who are persecuted for
  obeying the right! The kingdom of heaven
  belongs to you.
Happy are you when people hate you,
  exclude you, insult you, persecute you,
  and tell all kinds of evil lies about you,
  even banning your very name, on my
  account! Be glad and dance for joy,
  because your reward with God is great.
  Their ancestors did the very same things
  to the prophets before you.
But woe to you who are rich! You have
  already been paid in full.
Woe to you whose stomachs are stuffed!
  You will go hungry.
Woe to you who now laugh! You will be
  mourning and crying.
Woe to you when all people speak well of
  you! So did their ancestors to the false
  prophets.''

"You Are the Salt of the Earth and the Light of the World"

"You are the salt of the earth. Salt is a good thing, but if it loses its taste, there is no way to restore it. It is fit for neither the land nor the dungheap. It is no longer good for anything but to be thrown out and trampled underfoot. So listen if you have ears!

"You are the light of the world. A town on a hill cannot be hid. Nobody lights a lamp to put it in the cellar or under a bed or to cover it with a tub. Instead it is set on a stand, to give light to everybody in the house and to those entering. Let your light shine before people so that when they see the good you do they will give praise to your Father in heaven."

"The Law Says, But I Say"

"Do not think I have come to do away with the Law of Moses and the prophets' teachings. I did not come to abolish them. I came to complete them. I tell you, as long as heaven and earth last, not a letter, not even a dot will disappear from the Law until all that it stands for is accomplished.

"Whoever then relaxes even the least of these commandments and teaches others so, will have the lowest place in the kingdom of heaven. But anybody who keeps them and teaches others to do so will stand high in the kingdom of heaven. Remember this, unless your goodness surpasses that of the lawyers and the Pharisees, you won't ever get into the kingdom of heaven.

"You have learned that our forefathers were told, 'Don't commit murder. Anybody who commits murder must be brought to judgment.' But I tell you that everybody who nurses anger against a brother will be brought to judgment, whoever insults a brother must answer for it to the court, and whoever calls somebody else a fool stands in danger of hellfire! So if you find yourself at the altar with your offering and suddenly remember that one of your brethren has a grievance against you, leave your gift there in front of the altar and go be reconciled with that person first and then come back and offer your gift to God.

"You have heard it was said, 'Don't commit adultery.' But I tell you that everybody who looks at a woman with thoughts full of lust has already committed adultery with her in his heart.

"It was also said, 'Anybody who divorces his wife must give her a certificate of divorce.' But I tell you that any man who divorces his wife for any cause other than unfaithfulness involves her in adultery if she remarries, and the man who marries her commits adultery too.

"You have also heard our ancestors were told, 'Don't swear to a lie, but perform what you have sworn before the Lord.' But I tell you, don't swear at all, neither by heaven, because it is God's throne, nor by the earth, because it is his footstool, nor by Jerusalem, because it is the city of the Great King. And don't swear by your own head. You cannot even turn a hair of it white or black. A simple 'Yes' or 'No' is all you need to say. Anything beyond that comes from the evil one.

"You have heard it was said, 'An eye for an eye and a tooth for a tooth.' But I tell you, don't retaliate against the person who wrongs you. If anybody slaps you on the right cheek, turn and offer him the left as well. If anyone wants to sue you for your shirt, let him have your coat too. And if anyone forces you to go one mile, go with him two miles. Give to anybody who begs from you, and don't turn your back on the one who wants to borrow from you. When someone takes what is yours, don't demand it back. Always treat others as you would like them to treat you. That is the sum total of the Law and the prophets.

"You have heard it was said, 'Love your neighbor and hate your enemy.' But I tell you, love your enemies, do good to those who hate you, bless those who curse you, and pray for those who persecute you. Only in this way can you become children of your Father in heaven. He makes his sun shine on good and bad alike and sends rain on both the just and the unjust. If you love only those who love you, what reward have you got? Do not even the tax collectors do that? And if you do good only to those who do good to you and greet only your brethren, what have you done that's extraordinary? Even pagans do as much! If you lend only to those you expect to repay, what credit is that to you? Even sinners lend to each other if they are to be paid back in full. But love your enemies and do good to them and lend without expecting any return. You will have a great reward. You will be children of the Highest, because he himself is kind to the ungrateful and the bad. Be compassionate just as your Father in heaven is. You must be perfect like him."

"Avoid Religiosity"

"Be careful not to make a show of your religion before people. If you do, you won't have any reward from your heavenly Father.

"So when you make a gift for the poor, don't blow your horn, as the hypocrites do in the synagogues and on the streets, to win human praise. I am telling you the truth. They already have their reward. But when you give, don't even let your left hand know what your right hand is doing. Your gift must be in secret, and your Father who sees what is done in secret will reward you.

"Likewise when you fast, don't look dismal like the hypocrites. They go around with hungry faces to make sure people notice their fasting. Believe me, they've already got their reward. But when you fast, comb your hair and wash your face so that people can't tell you're fasting, but only your Father who is unseen. And your Father who sees what is secret will reward you.

"Again, when you pray, don't be like the hypocrites. They love to stand up and pray in the synagogues and at the street corners so that everybody will see them. I tell you, they have their reward. But when you pray, go into a room by yourself, lock the door, and pray to your Father secretly. And your Father who sees what is done in secret will reward you.

"Pray Simply"; the Parable of the Friend at Midnight

"And in praying don't heap phrase on phrase as the pagans do. They think that the more they say, the more likely they are to be heard. Don't imitate them. Your Father knows what you need before you ask him."

One of his disciples said, "Lord, teach us how to pray, just as John taught his disciples."

So he taught them, "When you pray, say,
    'Father,
    Your name be revered,
    Your kingdom come,
    And your will be done,
    On earth as well as in heaven.
    Give us today our daily bread,
    And forgive us our debts,

As we too have forgiven our debtors.
And don't bring us to the test,
But save us from the evil one.'
If you forgive others the wrongs they have done you, your Father in heaven will forgive you too, but if you do not forgive others, then neither will your Father forgive the wrongs you have done."

He added, "Imagine one of you who has a friend goes to him in the middle of the night and says, 'My friend, lend me three loaves. A friend of mine on a long trip has just dropped in on me, and I don't have a thing to serve him.' He replies from inside, 'Don't bother me. The door is locked for the night, and my children and I have gone to bed. I can't get up and give you anything.' Well, what then? I tell you, even if he won't get up and give him what he wants out of friendship, he will get up and give him all he needs just because the fellow keeps on asking.

"So I tell you, ask and you will receive, search and you will find, knock and the door will be opened to you. Everyone who asks will receive, whoever seeks will find, and to anyone who knocks, the door will be opened.

"Is there a father among you who would hand his child a stone when he asks for bread, a snake when he asks for fish, or a scorpion when he asks for an egg? If you then, bad as you are, know how to give your children what is good for them, how much more will your Father in heaven give good things to those who ask him!"

"You Cannot Serve Both God and Money"

"Don't store up for yourselves wealth on earth where moths and rust consume it and thieves break in to steal it. Sell all your belongings and give the money to the poor and provide yourselves purses that don't wear out. Save up your wealth in heaven where there is neither moth nor rust to spoil it and no thieves break in and steal. Your heart will always be where your riches are.

"Nobody can serve two masters. Either he will hate the one and love the other, or he will be devoted to the one and care nothing for the other. You cannot serve both God and money.

"So I tell you, don't worry about the necessities of life—whether you will have enough food and drink to keep you alive or clothes to cover your body. Surely life is more than just a matter of getting food, and the body more than just something to be clothed.

"Look at the crows. They neither plant nor harvest nor store in barns, yet your heavenly Father feeds them. Aren't you worth more than birds? Anyway, is there a single one of you who by worrying can add an inch to his height or a day to his life? If, then, you can't even manage such a little thing as that, why fret about the rest?

"And why worry about clothes? Look how the wild flowers grow in the fields. They don't work to make clothes for themselves. Yet I tell you, even Solomon in all his splendor was never dressed like one of these. But if that is how God clothes the wild grass, which is here today and gone tomorrow, burned up in the oven, won't he be all the more sure to clothe you, you people of little faith?

"So stop worrying yourselves sick asking, 'Where will our food come from?' 'What will we drink?' or 'Will we have anything to wear?' The heathen are always running after these things, but not you, because your heavenly Father knows you need them all.

"Don't be afraid, little flock. It is your Father's good pleasure to give you the kingdom! Seek first his kingdom and his virtue, and all the rest will come to you as well. Stop worrying about tomorrow. Tomorrow will look after itself. Each day has troubles enough of its own."

"Don't Judge Others"

"Do not pass judgment on others, and God will not judge you. Do not condemn others, and God will not condemn you. Forgive others, and God will forgive you. Give to others, and God will give to you. Good measure, pressed down, shaken together, and running over, will be poured in your lap. Remember, in the same way you judge others God will judge you, and whatever measure you deal out to others will be the measure dealt you in return.

"Why do you always look at the speck of sawdust in your brother's eye and never notice the log in your own? How can you say to him, 'My dear brother, let me take that speck out of your eye,' when you yourself are blind to the log in your own? You hypocrite! First take the log out of your own eye, and then you will see clearly to take the speck out of your brother's."

The True Wisdom

"Do not give dogs what is holy, and do not spread your pearls before pigs. They will only trample them underfoot and turn on you.

"Go in through the narrow gate. The gate is wide and the way easy that leads to destruction, and many travel that road. But the gate is narrow and the way hard that leads to life, and those who find it are few.

"Beware of false prophets—people who come to

you looking like sheep on the outside but are savage wolves on the inside. You will recognize them by their deeds. Every tree is known by its fruit. Can grapes be picked from a bramble bush or figs from a briar patch? In the same way a good tree always gives good fruit, and a poor tree bad fruit. The one cannot bear bad fruit, nor the other, good. And when a tree does not yield good fruit it is cut down and thrown on the fire. That is why I say you will know them by their fruits.

"Why do you call me 'Lord, Lord,' but do not do what I tell you? Not everybody who calls me 'Lord, Lord' will enter the kingdom of heaven, but only those who do the will of my heavenly Father. When that day comes, many will say to me, 'Lord, Lord, didn't we prophesy in your name, cast out devils in your name, and in your name perform many miracles?' Then I will tell them to their faces, 'I never knew you. Out of my sight, you wrongdoers!'

"What then of the one who hears these words of mine and acts on them? I will tell you what he is like. He is like a man who in building his house had the sense to dig deep and lay the foundation on solid rock. The rain fell, and the floods came, and the winds blew and beat on that house, but it did not fall because its foundation was sound.

"But what of the one who hears these words of mine and does not act on them? He is like a man who was foolish enough to build his house on sand. The rains poured down, the rivers flooded over, and the winds blew and buffeted that house, and down it came with a crash!"

When Jesus had finished speaking he came down from the mountain, and great crowds followed him. The people were astounded at his teaching, because unlike their lawyers he taught as if he himself were the authority.

The Centurion's Servant

As he entered Capernaum some Jewish elders approached him, sent by a centurion. The centurion had a servant he valued highly, who was at home in bed paralyzed and racked with pain, near death. Hearing about Jesus, he had sent these Jews with the request that Jesus come and save his servant's life.

They begged Jesus earnestly, "This man really deserves your help. He is a friend of our nation and the one who built us our synagogue."

Jesus agreed to go with them, but he was not far from the house when the centurion sent friends to tell him, "Sir, don't trouble yourself. I am not worthy to have you come under my roof, and that is why I did not presume to come to you in person. Just say the word and my servant will get well. I know, because in my position I myself am under orders, with soldiers under my command. I tell this one, 'Go!', and he goes; that one, 'Come here!', and he comes; and my slave, 'Do this!', and he does it."

Jesus listened to them in amazement, then turned to the crowd following him. "I tell you, nowhere, not even in Israel, have I found faith like this. Believe me, many people will come from east and west to feast with Abraham, Isaac, and Jacob in the kingdom of heaven, but those who were born to the kingdom will be thrown out in the dark—the place of wailing and gritting of teeth."

Then he sent this message to the centurion. "Because of your faith, so let it be." And the messengers returned home and found the servant back in good health. He was healed that very hour.

The Widow's Son at Nain

Soon afterwards Jesus went to a town called Nain, accompanied by his disciples and a large crowd. As he approached the gate of the town he met a funeral procession. The dead man was the only son of his widowed mother, and many of the townspeople were there with her.

When Jesus saw her his heart went out to her, and he said, "Don't cry any more." He stepped forward and put his hand on the bier, and the pallbearers halted. Then he spoke.

"Young man, I tell you, get up!" The dead man sat up and began to talk, and Jesus gave him back to his mother.

A deep awe fell on all the bystanders, and they praised God. "A great prophet has appeared among us! God has visited his people!" And the story of what he had done spread throughout Judea and all the surrounding country.

Messengers From John the Baptist

John in prison heard from his disciples what Jesus was doing and, summoning two of them, sent them to Jesus with this question. "Are you the one to come, or should we expect somebody else?"

While they were present Jesus cured many suffering from diseases, plagues, and evil spirits, and to many blind people he restored sight. And he gave them this answer. "Go back and tell John what you have seen and heard—how the blind recover their sight, the lame walk, the lepers are cured, the deaf hear, the dead are raised to life, and the good news is preached to the poor. And happy is the man who does not take offense at me!"

After John's messengers had left, Jesus began to speak about him to the crowds. "What did you go out in the desert to look at? A reed whistling in the wind? No? Then what did you go out to see? A man dressed in silks and satins? Quite the contrary, those who wear gorgeous clothes and live in luxury are to be found in kings' palaces. Tell me, then, what did you expect to see? A prophet? Yes indeed, and far more than a prophet. He is the man of whom it is written, 'Here is my herald, whom I send on ahead of you, and he will prepare the way for you.'

"I tell you there has never been a man born greater than John, yet the least one in the kingdom of God is greater than he is. All the prophets and the Law predicted the kingdom until John appeared, and if you will only believe their message he is Elijah, whose coming was promised. Since then, it is the good news of the kingdom that is being preached, and everyone forces his way in. The kingdom of heaven is being subjected to assault, and violent men are trying to seize it. Listen then if you have ears!"

When they heard him all the people, including the tax collectors, praised God. They had accepted John's baptism. But the Pharisees and the lawyers, having refused his baptism, rejected God's purpose for themselves.

"How can I describe the people of this day and age?" Jesus asked. "What are they like? They are like children playing games in the marketplace, shouting at each other. 'We played a tune for you, but you would not dance. So we wept and wailed, but you would not mourn!' John the Baptist came fasting and abstaining from wine, and you said, 'He is possessed!' Then comes the Son of Man eating and drinking, and you say, 'Look at him! A glutton and a drunkard, a friend of tax collectors and sinners!' Yet God's wisdom is proved right by its results."

"I Will Give You Rest"

"Come to me, all you who labor under heavy burdens, and I will give you rest. Take my yoke on your shoulders and learn from me. I am gentle and humble of heart, and you will find rest for your souls. My yoke is easy to bear, and my burden is light."

The Penitent Prostitute; the Parable of the Two Debtors

One of the Pharisees invited Jesus to dine with him, and he went to the Pharisee's house and took his place at the table. A woman in that town who was living an immoral life had learned that Jesus was dining at the Pharisee's house, so she brought an alabaster flask containing oil of myrrh and knelt down behind him, sobbing. She began to wet his feet with her tears and dried them with her hair, kissing them and anointing them with the myrrh.

When his host the Pharisee saw this, he said to himself, "If this man were really a prophet he would have known who this woman is, touching him, and what sort of woman she is—a sinner!"

"Simon," Jesus said to him, "I have something to say to you."

"What is it, Teacher?"

"Two men were in debt to a money-lender. One owed him five hundred denarii; the other, fifty. As neither one of them could pay, he let both off. Now which one of the two will love him more?"

"The one, I suppose, who was forgiven the larger debt."

"You are right."

Then turning towards the woman, Jesus said to Simon, "You see this woman? I came to your house and you gave me no water for my feet, but this woman has washed my feet with her tears and wiped them with her hair. You gave me no welcoming kiss, but from the time I came in she has not stopped kissing my feet. You provided no oil for my head, but she has covered my feet with perfume. So I tell you, her great love shows how much she has been forgiven. Her sins are many. But whoever is forgiven little loves little."

Then he said to the woman, "Your sins are forgiven."

The other guests began to ask themselves, "Who is this that he can forgive sins?" But he told the woman, "Your faith has saved you. Go in peace."

The Women Who Provided Support

After this Jesus went traveling from town to town and village to village, proclaiming the good news of the kingdom of God. With him were the twelve and also a number of women who had been set free from evil spirits and infirmities—Mary known as the Magdalene, from whom seven evil spirits had been driven out; Joanna the wife of Chuza, Herod's superintendent; Susanna; and many others. These women provided for them out of their own resources.

Jesus Accused of Alliance With the Devil

He came home, and once more such a crowd collected around them they could not even eat. When his family heard of this they set out to take charge of him, because people were saying he was out of his mind.

At this time a man was brought to him, possessed by an evil spirit so that he was both blind and speechless, and Jesus cured him, restoring both speech and sight. All the people were amazed and said, "Could this be the Son of David?" But the lawyers who had come down from Jerusalem and the Pharisees said, "He is possessed by Beelzebub," and "It is only by the help of Beelzebub the prince of demons that he is able to cast out demons."

Knowing their thoughts, Jesus said, "Every kingdom divided against itself is overrun and laid waste, and no town or household divided against itself can stand. So how can Satan drive out Satan? If he does, he is in rebellion against himself, his kingdom is divided and can't stand, and that is the end of him.

"If it is Beelzebub who gives me power to cast out demons, who gives your own people power to drive them out? If that is your argument, your own followers will prove you wrong.

"But if it is the Spirit of God who gives me power to cast out demons, then you can be sure the kingdom of God is already on you. How can anybody break into a strong man's house and make off with his goods without first tying him up? When such a man fully armed is on guard his possessions are safe. It is only when somebody stronger attacks and defeats him and carries off his arms and armor that his house can be ransacked and the plunder divided. Whoever is not with me must be against me, and whoever does not help me gather is really scattering.

"So I tell you, there is no sin, no blasphemy, that cannot be forgiven, except words deliberately spoken against the Holy Spirit, and they will not be forgiven. Whoever speaks a word against the Son of Man will be forgiven, but whoever speaks against the Holy Spirit will not be forgiven, now or hereafter. He has committed an eternal sin." (Jesus said this because of their charge that he was possessed by a demon.)

"To get good fruit you need a healthy tree. Grow a bad tree and you get bad fruit. You can tell a tree by its fruit. You snakes! How can your words be good when you yourselves are evil? Out of the abundance of the heart come the words of the mouth. A good person produces good out of the goodness stored up within him, and an evil one, from the evil inside him, produces evil.

"I tell you, on the day of judgment people will have to account for every thoughtless word that has passed their lips. By the words of your own mouth you will be acquitted or condemned.

"When an evil spirit has gone out of a person it wanders over the deserts looking for a resting place, and finding none, it says, 'I will go back to the home I left.' When it returns and finds the house vacant, clean, and orderly, off it goes and gets seven other spirits even worse than itself, and they all come in and settle down. So in the end that person is worse off than he was in the beginning. And that is how it will be with this evil generation."

"Show Us a Sign!"

At this some of the lawyers and Pharisees sought to put him to a test. "Teacher, just show us some portent from heaven."

He answered, "It is a wicked, godless generation that demands a sign! No sign will be given but the sign of the prophet Jonah. Just as Jonah spent three days and three nights in the whale's belly, the Son of Man will be three days and three nights in the heart of the earth. Just as Jonah became a sign to the Ninevites, so will the Son of Man be to this day and age.

"At the judgment when the people of today are on trial, the people of Nineveh will stand up and condemn them, because they repented at the preaching of Jonah and, look, what is here is greater than Jonah! On that day the Queen of the South will get up and condemn this generation, because she came from the ends of the earth to hear the wisdom of Solomon and, look, what is here is greater than Solomon!"

"Who Are My Mother and Brothers?"

As he said this a woman in the crowd called out, "How happy is the womb that carried you and the breasts that nursed you!"

"No!" he called back. "Happy are those who hear the word of God and keep it!"

He was still speaking to the people when his mother and brothers arrived outside, asking to speak to him. They were unable to reach him because of the crowd.

Someone told him, "Your mother and your brothers are here to see you. They're waiting outside."

Jesus turned to the man who told him. "Who is my mother? Who are my brothers?" Then looking around at those sitting in the circle in front of him, and pointing to his disciples, he said, "Look! Here are my mother and brothers! Whoever hears the word of God and does his will is my brother, my sister, my mother."

The Parable of the Sower

The same day Jesus left the house and began to teach beside the lake of Galilee. The crowd that gathered about him was so large he had to get into a boat. There he sat, with the whole crowd on the beach right down to the water's edge. And he taught them many things by means of parables.

"Listen! A man went out to sow his field with seed. As he scattered the seed some of it fell along the footpath where it got stepped on, and the birds came and ate it up. Other seed fell on rocky ground where it had little soil, and it sprouted quickly because the soil was lacking in depth. When the sun came up the young plants were scorched, and having no roots to speak of, they withered. Still other seed fell among thorns which grew up and choked the plants, and they yielded no grain. But some of the seed fell into good ground where it came up and grew and bore grain, and the yield was thirtyfold, sixtyfold, even a hundredfold." And he added, "Whoever has ears to hear with, listen!"

When Jesus was alone those around him with the twelve questioned him about the parables. He replied, "To you it has been given to see the secret of the kingdom of God, but to outsiders everything is just so many stories. So take note of what you hear. To the one with something, more will be given until he has enough and to spare, but from the one who is lacking, even what little he has will be taken away.

"They look without seeing and listen without hearing or understanding. There's a prophecy of Isaiah being fulfilled in them:

     'You will listen and listen but never
       understand.
     You will look and look but never see.
     This people's mind has grown dull.
     They have stopped up their ears
       and shut their eyes,

To keep from seeing with their eyes
and hearing with their ears
And understanding with their minds
and turning for me to heal them.'
"Don't you understand this parable? Then how are you going to understand any of them? Listen then and learn what the parable of the sower means.

"The seed he sows is the word of the kingdom of God. Those along the footpath are people in whom the word is sown but who do not understand it, and no sooner have they heard it than the evil one comes along and snatches away what has been sown in their minds, to keep them from believing and being saved.

"It is the same with those who receive the seed on rocky ground. As soon as they hear the word they accept it joyfully, but it strikes no root in them. They lack staying-power. They last for a while, but when trouble or persecution comes along on account of the word they fall away at once.

"Still others receive the seed among thorns. They hear the word, but the cares of this world, the false glamor of riches, and the desire for other things crowd in and choke the word, and it proves unfruitful.

"Then there are those who receive the seed in good soil. These are people who hear the word and understand it, who hold it fast in a good and honest heart, and who by patience and perseverance yield a harvest, some thirtyfold, some sixtyfold, some even a hundredfold."

The Parable of the Growing Seed

"The kingdom of God is like this. A man scatters seed over his field. He sleeps at night and is up and about during the day, and all the while the seeds are sprouting and growing. How, he does not know. The ground produces a crop by itself, first the blade, then the ear, then the full grain in the ear. But as soon as the grain is ripe he sets to work with his sickle, because harvest time has come."

The Parables of the Weeds, the Mustard Seed, the Yeast, the Buried Treasure, the Pearl, and the Net Full of Fish

Here is another parable he put before the crowds. "The kingdom of heaven is like this. A man sowed his field with good seed, but one night while everybody was asleep his enemy came, sowed weeds among the wheat, and made off. When the wheat came up and began to fill out, the weeds showed up too. The master's servants went to him and said, 'Sir, didn't you sow good seed in your field? Then how come it has weeds?' He replied, 'This is an enemy's doing.' 'Well then,' they said, 'shall we go pull up the weeds?' But he said, 'No. In gathering the weeds you might root up the wheat along with them. Let both grow together until harvest time, then I will tell the harvesters, "Gather the weeds first and tie them in bundles to be burned, then collect the wheat and put it in my barn." ' "

Here is still another one. "How shall we picture the kingdom of God? What parable can we use to illustrate it? It is like a mustard seed, which a man took and sowed in his field. It is the smallest of all seeds, but when full-grown it is the biggest of plants. It puts out such big branches the birds come nest in them."

He told them another parable. "The kingdom of heaven is like yeast. A woman takes it and mixes it with a bushel of flour until the whole batch of dough rises."

With many such parables Jesus presented his message to the crowds—as much as they were capable of receiving. He never spoke to them except by means of parables, but he explained everything privately to his disciples. The words of the prophet thus came true:

"I will open my mouth to speak in parables.
I will tell what has been hidden since the
world was made."

He then left the crowd and went indoors, where his disciples came to him and asked him to explain the parable of the weeds in the wheatfield. This was his answer.

"The man who sowed the good seed is the Son of Man. The field is the world. The good seed stands for the children of the kingdom; the weeds, for those who belong to the evil one. The enemy who sowed the weeds is the devil. The harvest is the end of the age. The harvesters are angels. So just as weeds are gathered and burned, at the end of the age the Son of Man will send out his angels, who will gather out of his kingdom everything that causes offense and all those whose deeds are evil, and these will be thrown into the blazing furnace—the place of wailing and gritting of teeth. But the righteous will shine like the sun in their Father's kingdom. Whoever has ears, listen!

"The kingdom of heaven is like treasure a man found buried in a field. He covers it up again and in great joy goes and sells everything he has and buys that field.

"Again, the kingdom of heaven is like a merchant on the lookout for fine pearls. Finding one that's priceless, he goes and sells everything he has and buys it.

"Again, the kingdom of heaven is like a net let down in the lake, and fish of every kind are caught in it. When it is full the men drag it ashore. Then they sit down and sort the good fish into buckets and throw the worthless ones away. That is how it will be at the end of the age. The angels will go out and separate the evil from the good and throw the evil into the blazing furnace—the place of wailing and gritting of teeth. Have you understood all this?"

"Yes," they answered.

"You see, when a teacher of the Law has become a learner in the kingdom of heaven, he is like a householder who can produce from his store both the new and the old."

Having finished these parables, he left.

"Even the Wind and Waves Obey Him"

That day in the evening Jesus, seeing himself surrounded by a great crowd, said to his disciples, "Let's cross over to the other side of the lake." So they left the crowd and took him with them in the boat in which he had been sitting. Other boats were there too.

A heavy squall came on, and the waves broke over the boat until it was all but swamped. Jesus was in the stern asleep on a cushion. The disciples aroused him with their cries.

"Master, save us! We're about to die! The boat is sinking! Don't you care?"

He stood up and rebuked the wind, "Be quiet!", and said to the sea, "Be still!" The wind died down, and there was a dead calm.

Then he said to them, "Why are you so scared, you people of little faith? Have you not learned to trust yet?"

They were filled with awe and said to each other, "What kind of man is this? He gives orders to the wind and the waves, and even they obey him!"

The Gerasene Madman

They came to the other side of the lake, opposite Galilee, into the country of the Gerasenes (or Gergesenes, or Gadarenes). As Jesus stepped ashore he encountered a man of that town who was demon-possessed, coming out from among the tombs where he lived. He had gone for a long time without clothes and was so fierce that nobody dared travel that way. No one could control him any more. Even chains were useless. He had often been chained up and put in irons, but he had snapped the chains and broken the irons. And nobody was strong enough to subdue him. Night and day he wandered among the tombs and over the hillsides, crying and cutting himself on the rocks.

When he saw Jesus in the distance he ran and threw himself down in front of him, screaming out loud, "Jesus, Son of the Highest God! What do you want with me? In God's name don't torment me!" (He said this because Jesus was already demanding, "You evil spirit, come out of this man!")

"What is your name?" Jesus asked him.

"My name is Legion, there are so many of us!" And he begged Jesus not to banish them from the country to the abyss.

There happened to be a large herd of pigs nearby, feeding on the hillside. The demons begged Jesus, "If you cast us out, send us among the pigs. Let us go into them."

"Go then."

The spirits came out of the man and went into the pigs, and the herd, numbering about two thousand, stampeded down the steep bank into the lake and drowned.

When the herdsmen saw what happened they took to their heels and carried the news to both town and countryside, and the people came out to see. Coming up to Jesus they saw the madman who had been possessed by the legion of devils, sitting there at Jesus' feet, clothed and in his right mind. The spectators told them how the madman had been cured and what had happened to the pigs. They were frightened and begged Jesus to leave their district.

As he was stepping into the boat, the man who had been possessed asked to go with him. Jesus would not allow it but told him, "Go back home to your own people and tell them what God in his mercy has done for you." So the man went off and spread the news of what Jesus had done for him all through the Ten Towns, and everyone was amazed.

Jairus' Daughter and the Woman With the Hemorrhage

When Jesus returned by boat to the other shore a great crowd welcomed him. They had all been waiting for him.

While he was at the lakeside the president of one of the synagogues came up, Jairus by name. His only daughter, about twelve years old, was dying. When he saw Jesus he threw himself down at his feet and pleaded with him.

"My little daughter is at death's door. I beg you to come lay your hands on her, so she will get well and live."

Jesus started off with him, but so many people were going along too that they were crowding him on every side. Among them was a woman who had suffered from severe bleeding for twelve years. Despite endless treatments by doctors on which she had spent everything she had, nobody had been able to cure her. In fact she had grown worse.

Having heard what people were saying about Jesus, she came up from behind in the crowd and touched the fringe of his cloak. "If I just touch his clothes," she said to herself, "I shall get well." At once her hemorrhage stopped, and she realized her trouble was gone.

At the same time Jesus, aware that power had gone out of him, turned around in the crowd and asked, "Who was it that touched me?"

"Master," his disciples answered, "you see the crowd is pressing in on you from all sides, so how can you ask, 'Who touched me?' "

Jesus, however, looking around to see who had done it, replied, "Someone did touch me. I felt power go out of me."

The woman, realizing she had been detected, came trembling and fell at his feet and told him the whole truth. "My daughter," he said to her, "your faith has made you well. Go in peace, free forever from this trouble."

While he was still speaking, a message came from the official's house. "Your daughter is dead. Why trouble the Rabbi further?" But Jesus, overhearing the message, told Jairus, "Don't be afraid. Just believe, and she will be well again."

He let no one go on with him beyond this point except Peter and James and James' brother John. They arrived to find the house in a tumult. Everybody was weeping and wailing for the girl. He noticed that even the musicians for the funeral were already there.

"Why all this crying and commotion?" Jesus said to them. "The child isn't dead. She's asleep."

They laughed at him, knowing full well she was dead. He, however, turned them all out and, accompanied only by the father and mother and his own companions, went into the room in which the child was lying.

Taking her by the hand, he said to her, *"Talitha cum,"* which means, "Little girl, get up!" She got up immediately and walked about.

At this her parents were beside themselves with amazement, but he told them to give her something to eat and gave them strict orders to let no one hear about it. Nevertheless the news of this spread all over that part of the country.

The Blind See and the Dumb Speak

As Jesus passed on from there he was followed by two blind men who cried out, "Son of David, take pity on us!" After he had gone indoors they came up to him.

"Do you believe I can do what you want?" Jesus asked them.

"Yes, sir."

He touched their eyes and said, "Then let it happen just as you believe!" And their eyes were opened.

Jesus gave them strict orders, "See to it nobody learns of this!" But they went out and spread his fame far and wide.

While the men were on their way out a fellow was brought to him who was speechless because he was possessed by a devil. As soon as the demon was driven out, the man started talking. Amazed, the crowds exclaimed, "We've never seen the like of this in Israel!" But the Pharisees said, "He drives out devils by the prince of devils."

The Last Visit to Nazareth

Jesus went back to his own country, accompanied by his disciples. On the Sabbath day he began to teach in the synagogue, and the many people who heard him were surprised and asked, "How did he come by this wisdom and these miraculous powers? Is he not the carpenter, Mary's boy, and the brother of James, Joseph, Simon, and Judas? And are not all his sisters living here? Then where did he get all this?"

So they took offense at him. This led Jesus to say, "No prophet goes without honor except in his own country and among his own kin and in his own house."

Apart from laying his hands on a few sick people and healing them he worked no miracles there, so surprising was their lack of faith.

The Mission of the Twelve

Jesus went through all the towns and villages teaching in their synagogues, announcing the good news of the Kingdom, and curing all kinds of ailment and disease. When he saw the crowds his heart was moved to pity, because they were harassed and helpless like sheep without a shepherd. He told his disciples, "The harvest is great, but the workers are scarce. So pray the Lord of the harvest to send out more workers to harvest his crop."

He called the twelve together, paired them off, and sent them out to proclaim the kingdom of God and to heal. He gave them authority to drive out demons and to cure every kind of ailment and disease. To these twelve Jesus gave the following instructions.

"Don't take the road to Gentile lands and don't

enter any Samaritan town. Go instead to the lost sheep of the house of Israel. And as you go, proclaim the message, 'The kingdom of heaven is at hand!' Heal the sick, raise the dead, make the lepers clean, cast out devils. You received without cost, so give without charge.

"Take nothing with you for the trip, no bread or beggar's bag, and no money in your belts. You can take a walking stick and wear sandals, but don't even take a spare coat. The worker earns his keep.

"When you come to any town or village, look for some worthy person in it and make your home with him until you leave. As you enter a house, say 'Peace be with you.' If it is worthy, let your peace remain there. If it is unworthy, take back your blessing. If anyone refuses to welcome you or listen to what you say, then as you leave that house or that town shake the dust of it off your feet. This will be a warning to them! I tell you it will be more tolerable on the day of judgment for the land of Sodom and Gomorrah than for that town.

"Listen! I send you out like sheep among wolves, so be as wary as snakes and as innocent as doves. No pupil outranks his teacher, or a servant his master. The pupil should be content to share his teacher's lot, and the servant his master's. If they have called the master Beelzebub, how much worse slander will they heap on his household!

"Don't be afraid of them. There is nothing covered up that won't be uncovered, nothing hidden that won't be made known. What I tell you in the dark, repeat in broad daylight, and what you hear whispered, shout from the housetops! To you my friends I say, do not fear those who kill the body but after that can do nothing more. I will tell you whom to fear. Fear the one who after killing has authority to throw into hell. Believe me, he is the one to be afraid of!

"Are not two sparrows sold for a penny, and five for two? Yet without your Father's permission not one of them can fall to the ground. As for you, even the hairs of your head have all been counted. So don't be afraid. You are worth far more than any number of sparrows.

"Whoever then acknowledges me before people, the Son of Man will acknowledge before God's angels, but whoever disowns me before people, I shall disown before my Father in heaven. No person is worthy of me who cares more for father or mother than he does for me. Nobody is worthy of me who cares more for son or daughter. And no one is worthy of me who doesn't take up his cross and walk in my footsteps. By saving his life a person will lose it. By losing his life for my sake he will gain it.

"To welcome you is the same as welcoming me, and whoever welcomes me welcomes the one who sent me. Whoever receives a prophet because he is a prophet will be given a prophet's reward, and whoever receives a good man because he is a good man will be given a good man's reward. And if anybody gives so much as a cup of cold water to one of the least of these my followers because he is my follower, believe me, that person surely won't go unrewarded."

When Jesus had finished giving his twelve disciples their instructions he left that place and went to teach and preach in the neighboring towns. The disciples set out and traveled from village to village, calling publicly for repentance and proclaiming the good news. They drove out many devils, and many sick people they anointed with oil and cured.

John Is Beheaded

Herod the prince heard about all this, Jesus' fame having spread, and was unsure what to make of it, because some people were saying, "John the Baptist has come back to life! That is why these miraculous powers are at work in him." Others were saying, "It's Elijah." Still others were saying, "It is a prophet like one of the prophets of old."

Herod said, "As for John, I had him beheaded myself, but who's this I hear such talk about? Can it be that John has come back from the dead?" And he was anxious to see Jesus.

This same Herod had ordered John's arrest and put him in prison at the instance of his brother Philip's wife, Herodias, whom Herod had married. John had told him, "It isn't legal for you to marry your brother's wife!" Herodias therefore nursed a grudge against John and wanted to have him killed. But she was unable because Herod was overawed by John, knowing him to be a good and holy man and that the people were convinced he was a prophet. And Herod was afraid of the people. So he kept him in custody. He liked to listen to John although the listening left him greatly perplexed.

Herodias found her opportunity when Herod's birthday arrived. He gave a banquet for his chief officials and commanders and the leading men of Galilee. Her daughter came in and danced for them and delighted Herod and his guests so much that the king said to the girl, "Ask anything you want and I shall give it to you." He even swore on his oath, "Whatever you ask I shall give you, even half my kingdom!"

She went out and asked her mother, "What shall I ask for?"

"The head of John the Baptist," Herodias said.

The girl hurried back at once to the king with her request. "I want you to give me here and now on a platter the head of John the Baptist."

The king was taken aback, but out of regard for the oath he had sworn in front of his guests he could not bring himself to refuse her. So he sent a soldier of the guard with orders to bring John's head. The soldier went and cut off John's head in prison, brought the head on a platter, and gave it to the girl who took it to her mother.

When John's disciples heard the news they came and took his body away and laid it in a tomb, then they went and told Jesus.

IV

The Training of the Twelve
In and Around Galilee

The Feeding of the Five Thousand

The messengers now rejoined Jesus and reported to him everything they had done and taught, but so many people were coming and going that they could not even eat in peace.

He told them, "Let's go off by ourselves to some quiet place where we can be alone and you can get some rest." So they set off privately by boat for a deserted spot on the other side of the Sea of Galilee—the Sea of Tiberias. (Jesus was going to take them and retire to a town called Bethsaida.)

Many people, however, saw them leave and recognized them. So the crowds found out, and they followed because they had seen the signs he performed in healing the sick. They came around by land, hurrying from all the towns to the place toward which Jesus and his disciples were heading, and arrived there first.

When he came ashore he saw the great throng, and his heart went out to them because they were like sheep without a shepherd. So he welcomed them and began to teach them many things about the kingdom of God and cured those in need of healing.

As the day wore on, Jesus went up the hillside and sat down with his disciples. It was near the time of Passover—the great Jewish festival.

"This is a deserted spot," his disciples reminded him, "and it's getting very late. You had better send the people off to the farms and villages round about, to buy themselves something to eat."

"There is no need for them to go. You give them something to eat."

"Do you want us to go spend 200 denarii on bread to give them a meal?"

Looking up and seeing the throng approaching, Jesus asked Philip, "How are we going to buy enough bread to feed all these people?" (He said this to try Philip out. Actually, he already knew what he was going to do.)

"Two hundred denarii," Philip answered, "wouldn't even buy enough bread for each of them to have just a little."

"How many loaves have you got? Go see."

Andrew, Simon Peter's brother, returned and told Jesus, "There's a boy here with five barley loaves and two fish, but what does that amount to, divided among so many people?"

"Bring them here to me, and have the people sit down in groups on the grass."

So the men sat down in rows, in a hundred groups

of fifty each. Then taking the five loaves and two fish, Jesus looked up to heaven and gave thanks, broke the loaves into pieces, and gave them to the disciples to distribute. He did the same with the fish, and all of them ate to their hearts' content.

When everyone had had enough he told his disciples, "Collect the pieces left over, so nothing is lost." This they did, and twelve great baskets full of scraps were picked up from the leftovers of the bread and fish. And the number of men who had eaten was about five thousand, not counting the women and children.

Jesus Comes to His Disciples
Across Stormy Waters

When the people saw the sign Jesus had performed, the word went around, "This is really the prophet! The one to come into the world!"

Jesus immediately told his disciples to embark and cross to Bethsaida ahead of him while he himself got rid of the crowd. He was aware that the people were on the verge of coming and seizing him to proclaim him king. Taking leave of them, he went off up the hillside alone to pray.

Evening had come when the disciples got down to the sea, embarked, and started across toward Capernaum. It was now dark, and the boat was already well out on the water, while Jesus was by himself on the land.

Sometime between three and six in the morning, seeing them laboring at the oars against a strong headwind and a rough sea, he came toward them walking on the water. He was going to pass them by, but they saw him walking on the lake. They cried out in terror, thinking it was a ghost. He spoke to them at once.

"Take courage! I am. Don't be afraid."

Peter called to him, "Lord, if it is really you, tell me to come to you over the water."

"Come on!"

Peter stepped out of the boat and started to walk over the water to Jesus. But seeing the strength of the gale, he was gripped by fear, and beginning to sink, he cried out, "Lord! Save me!"

Quickly Jesus reached out and grabbed him. "Why did you doubt? What little faith you've got!"

They climbed aboard and the wind died down. The disciples were completely dumbfounded. They had not understood the incident of the loaves. Their minds were closed to its significance.

The boat immediately reached the shore they were making for, and they landed and made fast there. The place was Gennesaret.

As they came ashore he was recognized immediately. And people scoured the whole countryside and brought the sick on stretchers to any place he was reported to be. Wherever he went, to farmsteads, villages, or towns, they laid out the sick in the marketplaces and begged him just to let them touch the fringe of his cloak. And all those who touched him were cured.

"I Am the Real Bread"

The next morning after the crossing the crowd was standing on the opposite shore. They had seen only one boat there, and Jesus they knew had not embarked with his disciples, who had gone away without him. Boats from Tiberias, however, came ashore near the place where the people had eaten the bread, and when the crowd saw that neither Jesus nor his disciples were there any longer, they got aboard these boats and headed for Capernaum in search of him.

Finding him on the other side, they asked him, "Rabbi, when did you come here?"

"I'm telling you the truth. You have come looking for me, not because you saw a miracle, but because you ate your fill of the bread. Don't work for this food that spoils but for the food that lasts—the food of eternal life. This other food the Son of Man will give you, because he is the one on whom the Father has set his approval."

"What must we do, to be doing God's work?"

"This is the work God requires. Believe in the one he has sent."

"What visible sign do you perform so we can believe you? What great work will you do? Our ancestors got manna to eat in the desert. As scripture says, 'He gave them bread from heaven to eat.'"

"I'm telling you the truth. It was not Moses who gave you the bread from heaven. My Father gives you the real bread from heaven. And God's bread is the bread that comes down from heaven and gives life to the world."

"Sir, give us this bread today and always."

"I am the bread that gives life. Whoever comes to me will never be hungry, and whoever believes in me will never be thirsty. But you, as I said, don't believe even though you have seen. Everyone the Father gives me will come to me, and anyone who comes to me I shall never turn away.

"I have come down from heaven, not to do my own will, but the will of the one who sent me. This is his will, that I should lose none of those he has given me but should raise them all to life on the last day. This is what my Father wants, that everyone who sees the Son and believes in him should possess eternal life. And I shall raise him up on the last day."

The Jews began to mutter in disapproval because he said, "I am the bread that came down from heaven." "This man," they said, "is Jesus son of Joseph, isn't he? We know his father and mother. So how can he say he came down from heaven?"

"Stop arguing among yourselves," Jesus told them. "Nobody can come to me unless he is drawn by the Father who sent me. And I shall raise him to life on the last day. It is written in the prophets, 'And they shall all be taught by God.' Everyone who has listened to the Father and learned from him comes to me. I don't mean anyone has seen the Father. The one come from God is the only one to have seen the Father.

"I am telling you the truth. The believer possesses eternal life. I am the bread of life. Your ancestors ate the manna in the desert but they died. If a person eats the bread I speak of, that comes down from heaven, he will not die. I am this living bread come down from heaven. If anyone eats this bread he will live forever. The bread I shall give is my own flesh. I give it for the life of the world."

This touched off a fierce dispute among the Jews. "How can this man give us his flesh to eat?"

"I am telling you the truth," Jesus replied. "Unless you eat the flesh of the Son of Man and drink his blood, you have no life in you. Whoever eats my flesh and drinks my blood possesses eternal life, and I shall raise him up on the last day. My flesh is the real food; my blood, the real drink. Whoever eats my flesh and drinks my blood lives in me and I in him. Just as the living Father sent me and I live because of the Father, whoever eats me will live because of me. This is the bread that came down from heaven, and it's not like the bread our ancestors ate. They are dead, but whoever eats this bread will live forever."

This was spoken in synagogue while Jesus was teaching at Capernaum. Many of Jesus' own disciples on hearing it exclaimed, "This is more than we can stomach! Why listen to such nonsense?"

Jesus was aware of their reaction and asked them, "Does this shock you? What if you were to see the Son of Man go back up where he was before? What gives life is the Spirit alone. Flesh is no help at all. The words I have spoken to you are both spirit and life. Yet some of you do not believe." (Jesus knew all along which ones did not believe and which one would betray him.) He kept saying, "This is why I told you nobody can come to me unless the Father makes it possible for him."

From that time on, many of his disciples withdrew and stopped following him. So Jesus asked the twelve, "Will you leave me too?"

Simon Peter answered for them. "Lord, to whom would we go? You have the words of eternal life. We have believed and come to know you are God's Holy One."

"I chose all twelve of you, right? Yet one is a devil!" (He meant Judas the son of Simon Iscariot. This was the one destined to hand Jesus over, and he was one of the twelve.)

After this, Jesus continued traveling around in Galilee. He wanted to avoid Judea because the Jews there were looking for a chance to kill him.

What Defiles a Person?

Once when Jesus had finished speaking, a Pharisee invited him to dinner, so he went in and sat down to eat.

A group of Pharisees and some lawyers who had come from Jerusalem gathered around. They were all aghast to notice that Jesus and some of his disciples were eating their food with "unclean" hands—in other words, without having washed them. (In obedience to the tradition of the elders, the Pharisees and the Jews in general never eat without washing their hands. On coming from the marketplace they never eat without first washing. And there are many other points on which they have a traditional rule to maintain, such as the washing of cups and jugs and copper bowls.)

These Pharisees and lawyers asked him, "Why do your disciples disobey the ancient tradition and eat their food with defiled hands?"

"Isaiah was right when he prophesied about you hypocrites:

'This people pays me lip service,
But their mind is far away from me.
They worship me in vain,
Because they teach as doctrines
the commandments of people.'

To maintain human tradition, you neglect God's commandment.

"You are experts at setting aside God's law in order to uphold your tradition! Moses commanded, 'Honor your father and your mother,' and again, 'Whoever curses his father or mother must be put to death.' But you hold that if anybody has something he could use to help his father or mother but tells them, 'This is *Corban*' (meaning 'set apart for God'), he is excused from helping them. Thus by your own tradition handed down among you, you set God's word at naught. And many other things you do are just like that."

He called the crowd to him once more and said to

them, "Listen to me, all of you, and understand this. It's not what goes into a person from the outside that defiles him, but what comes out. This defiles the person."

When he had left the people and gone indoors his disciples came and told him, "Do you realize the Pharisees were deeply offended by what you said?"

"Every plant not planted by my Father in heaven will be rooted up. Let them alone. They are blind guides, and if one blind man guides another both will fall in the ditch. A pupil can go no higher than his teacher, but everyone when his training is complete will reach his teacher's level."

Then Peter spoke up. "Tell us what the parable means."

"Are you as dull as the rest? Don't you see that nothing entering a person from the outside can defile him, because it enters, not his heart, but his stomach, and so passes on out of the body?" (Thus he declared all foods fit to eat.)

He went on, "It is what comes out of a person that defiles him. From the inside, out of the heart, come the evil thoughts that lead one to do immoral things, to rob, murder, and commit adultery—greed, malice, deceit, indecency, envy, slander, pride, and folly. All these evil things come from inside, and they are what defile a person. But to eat without first washing his hands, that cannot defile him."

The Gentile Woman's Daughter

Jesus then left that place and went off to the region around the cities of Tyre and Sidon. He found a house to stay in and would have liked to remain incognito, but this was impossible. Almost at once a woman whose young daughter was possessed by a demon heard about him, came in, and fell at his feet. She was a Gentile, a Phoenician Syrian by nationality.

"Son of David, sir!" she cried, "Take pity on me! My daughter is tormented by a devil." But he said not a word in reply.

His disciples came and urged him, "Send her away! See how she comes shouting after us."

"I was sent to the lost sheep of the house of Israel and to them alone."

The woman came back and fell at his feet and begged, "Help me, sir!"

"Let the children be satisfied first," he told her. "It is not right to take the children's bread and throw it to the dogs."

"True, sir, but even the dogs under the table are allowed to eat the scraps the children drop."

"Woman, what faith you've got! For saying that, go home content. The demon has gone out of your daughter."

Thus it happened. When she returned home she found the child lying in bed and the evil spirit gone.

The Deaf Mute

On his return journey to the Sea of Galilee from the region of Tyre Jesus went the long way around, through Sidon and the territory of the Ten Towns.

People brought him a man who was deaf and stammered, with the request that he lay his hands on him. Jesus took the man aside, away from the crowd, put his fingers into his ears, spat, and touched his tongue. Then looking up to heaven, he sighed and said to him, "*Ephphatha,*" which means, "Be opened."

With that the man's ears were opened, and at the same time his speech impediment was removed and he spoke plainly. Jesus ordered them not to tell anybody, but the more he forbade them the more they told it. Their astonishment knew no bounds. "Everything he does, he does well," they said. "He even makes the deaf hear and the dumb speak!"

The Feeding of the Four Thousand

Reaching the Sea of Galilee Jesus climbed up in the hills and sat down. Great crowds came bringing to his feet the lame, the maimed, the blind, the dumb, and many others, and he healed them. The throng was filled with wonder to see the dumb speak, the maimed whole, the lame walk, and the blind see, and they praised the God of Israel.

Since the crowd was without food, Jesus called his disciples. "I feel sorry for all these people. They have been with me now for three days and have nothing to eat. If I send them home hungry they may well faint on the road. Some of them have come a long way."

"How could anyone provide all these people with bread in this desert?" the disciples answered.

"How many loaves have you got?"

"Seven," they said.

He ordered the people to sit down on the ground. Then he took the seven loaves and after giving thanks to God broke the bread and gave it to his disciples to hand out, and they served it to the people. They also had a few small fish which he blessed and ordered them to distribute. Everyone had plenty to eat, and seven baskets of scraps were picked up. The people who ate numbered about four thousand men, besides women and children.

Then he dismissed the crowd and without delay got

into the boat with his disciples and went to the district of Dalmanutha (or Magadan).

"Beware of the Yeast of the Pharisees and Sadducees"

The Pharisees and Sadducees came out to test Jesus. They asked him to show them a portent from heaven.

He sighed deeply. "Why do the people of this day and age keep asking for a sign? It is an evil, godless generation that demands a sign. I tell you this. No sign will be given this generation but the sign of Jonah." With that he left them, reembarked, and started across to the other side of the lake.

Now they had forgotten to bring any extra bread. They had no more than one loaf in the boat.

Jesus began to warn them, "Be on your guard against the yeast of the Pharisees and Sadducees and of Herod."

"He says this because we didn't bring any bread," they began whispering among themselves.

Knowing what was on their minds, Jesus asked them, "Why do you talk about not having any bread? How little faith you have! Don't you have any inkling yet? Are your minds still closed? You have eyes. Can't you see? You've got ears. Can't you hear? Don't you remember how many baskets of leftovers you picked up when I broke the five loaves for the five thousand?"

"Twelve," they answered.

"And how many when I broke the seven loaves among the four thousand?"

"Seven," they said.

"And you still don't understand I was not talking about bread? Guard yourselves from the yeast of the Pharisees and Sadducees!"

They then began to get the idea that he was warning them to be on their guard, not against the yeast used in bread, but against the teaching of these men.

The Blind Man of Bethsaida

When they arrived at Bethsaida some people brought a blind man to Jesus and begged him to touch him. He took the blind man by the hand and led him away, out of the village. After spitting on the man's eyes Jesus placed his hands on him and asked him whether he could see anything. The man's sight began to return.

"I see people," he said. "They look like trees, but they are walking about."

Jesus put his hands on the man's eyes again, and this time the man looked hard and saw everything clearly. Then Jesus sent him home with the order, "Don't tell anyone in the village."

"Who Do You Say I Am?"

When he came to the territory of Philip's Caesarea Jesus after praying alone asked his disciples, "Who do people say I am?"

"Some say John the Baptist; others, Elijah; others, Jeremiah; and still others, that one of the old prophets has come back to life."

"And you, who do you say I am?"

Simon Peter answered, "You are the Messiah, the Son of the living God."

"Simon Bar-Jona, you are happy indeed! Flesh and blood did not reveal that to you, but my heavenly Father. And this I tell you. You are Peter, the Rock, and on this rock I shall build my church, and the gates of death will never close on it. I shall give you the keys of the kingdom of heaven. Whatever you forbid on earth will be forbidden in heaven, and whatever you allow on earth will be allowed in heaven." He then gave his disciples strict orders not to tell anyone he was the Messiah.

From that time on, Jesus began to teach them that the Son of Man had to go to Jerusalem and undergo great sufferings, be rejected by the elders, chief priests, and lawyers, and be put to death, and rise again on the third day. He spoke bluntly of these things.

Peter took him by the arm and began to rebuke him. "Heaven forbid, Lord! This will never happen to you!"

Jesus turned and, looking at his disciples, stopped Peter short with these words. "Get out of my way, Satan! You think as people think, not as God thinks."

Then he said to everybody, "If anyone wants to be a follower of mine he will have to leave self behind and take up his cross daily and walk in my footsteps. Whoever cares for his own safety is lost, but if a person will lose himself for my sake and that of the good news he will find his life.

"What does anyone gain by winning the whole world at the cost of his own soul? What can he offer that will buy it back? If anyone is ashamed of me and mine in this wicked and godless age the Son of Man will be ashamed of him when he comes in the glory of his Father and of his holy angels. Then he will give each one the due reward for what he has done."

He went on to say, "I tell you this. There are some standing here who will not taste death before they have seen the kingdom of God already come in power."

The Transfiguration

About a week after this conversation Jesus took Peter and the brothers James and John with him and led them up a high mountain by themselves to pray. While he was praying the appearance of his face changed. It was shining like the sun, and his clothes turned dazzling white, whiter than any bleach on earth could make them.

Suddenly two men were there in heavenly glory conversing with Jesus, speaking of his exodus—the destiny he was to fulfill at Jerusalem. They were Moses and Elijah.

Peter and his companions had been sound asleep when they woke up and saw Jesus' glory and the two men talking with him. Peter spoke.

"Rabbi, what a good thing we're here! We can make three tabernacles, one for you, one for Moses, and one for Elijah." (He really had no idea what to say, they were so terrified.)

The words were hardly out of his mouth when a bright cloud appeared and cast its shadow over them, and out of the cloud came a voice. "This is my own dear son, my chosen one, with whom I am delighted. Listen to him!"

At the sound of the voice the disciples fell on their faces in terror. Jesus came up and touched them.

"Stand up," he said. "Don't be afraid."

When they looked up they saw nobody but him.

On their way down the mountain he ordered them not to tell anyone what they had seen until the Son of Man had risen from the dead. They obeyed his order and in those days told no one anything of what they had seen. But among themselves they discussed what this "rising from the dead" could mean.

"Why do the lawyers say Elijah must be the first to come?" they asked Jesus.

"Yes, Elijah does come first to set everything right.

But I tell you Elijah has already come, and they failed to recognize him. They worked their will on him just as the scriptures predicted. In the same way the Son of Man must be rejected by the people of this day and age, endure great sufferings at their hands, and be treated with contempt." Then the disciples understood he meant John the Baptist.

The Epileptic Boy

When the four of them rejoined the rest of the disciples the next day they saw a large crowd around them. Some lawyers were arguing with them. The whole crowd was surprised to see Jesus and ran forward to welcome him.

"What is this argument all about?" he asked.

A man in the crowd came up and knelt down in front of him. "Master, I brought my only son who is an epileptic and speechless. Whenever he has an attack he suddenly cries out, and the spirit throws him to the ground in a fit. He foams at the mouth, grits his teeth, and goes rigid. I asked your disciples to drive the spirit out, but they were not able."

"What an unbelieving and perverse generation!" Jesus exclaimed. "How long am I to be with you? How long must I bear with you? Bring him here to me."

So they brought the boy to him. When the spirit saw him it threw the boy immediately into convulsions, and he rolled about on the ground foaming at the mouth.

"How long has he been like this?" Jesus asked his father.

"From childhood. Often it has almost made an end of him by throwing him into the fire or into water. He suffers terribly. If it's at all possible for you, take pity on us and help us."

"If it's possible!" exclaimed Jesus. "Everything is possible to one who believes."

"I do believe," cried the boy's father. "Please help my unbelief!"

Jesus noticed that the crowd was closing in on them, so he rebuked the evil spirit. "Deaf and dumb spirit, I command you, come out of him and never go back!"

After crying aloud and racking him from head to foot it came out, and the boy looked so much like a corpse that many people said, "He's dead." But Jesus took his hand and helped him to his feet. He was cured instantly. Then Jesus gave him back to his father, and all the people were amazed at God's mighty power.

After Jesus had gone indoors his disciples asked him privately, "Why couldn't we cast the demon out?"

"Only prayer can drive out this sort," he replied.

Faith Like a Mustard Seed

"Your faith is too weak," Jesus told his disciples.

"Strengthen our faith!" the messengers begged.

"Remember this," he told them. "If you have faith no bigger even than a mustard seed, you can say to this mountain, 'Move from here to there!' and it will go. Or to that sycamore tree, 'Root yourself up and replant yourself in the sea!' and it would obey you. Nothing will prove impossible for you."

Jesus Again Predicts His Death

They now left that district and made a journey through Galilee. Jesus wanted his whereabouts kept secret because he was teaching his disciples, "Don't forget what I am about to tell you. The Son of Man will be handed over to people who will kill him, and on the third day he will be raised to life."

They were greatly distressed but did not really understand what he was saying and were afraid to ask. Its meaning was hidden from them to keep them from grasping its full import.

The Temple Tax

On their arrival at Capernaum the collectors of the Temple tax came up to Peter and asked, "Doesn't your teacher pay Temple tax?"

"Of course," said Peter.

When he went indoors Jesus forestalled him by asking, "What do you think about this, Simon? From whom do earthly monarchs collect tax or toll? From their own children or from others?"

"From others," replied Peter.

"Why then the children are exempt! But we don't want to give offense, so go cast a line in the lake. Take the first fish that comes to the hook, open its mouth, and you will find a shekel. Take that and pay it in. It will meet the tax for both of us."

"Who Will Be Greatest in God's Kingdom?"

When they were settled indoors at Capernaum Jesus asked his disciples, "What were you arguing about on the road?" But they were silent because on the way they had been disputing which one of them was the greatest.

He sat down and called the twelve to him and said, "Whoever wants to be first must make himself last of all and servant of all."

Then he called a little child, set him in front of them, put his arms around him, and said, "Remember this. Unless you change and become like children you will never get into the kingdom of heaven. Let a person humble himself until he is like this child, and he will be the greatest in the kingdom of heaven. Whoever is the least among all of you is the greatest.

"Everyone will be salted with fire. Salt is a good thing, but if it loses its taste how would you season it? So have salt in yourselves and be at peace with each other."

"Guard Yourselves and the Children From Temptation"

He continued, "Whoever welcomes one such child in my name welcomes me, and whoever receives me receives not me but the one who sent me. And as for the person who causes one of these little ones to sin who believe in me, it would be better for him to be thrown out in the deep sea with a big millstone tied around his neck!

"How sad for the world that there are temptations to sin. Come they must, but woe betide the one through whom they come. So watch out! If your right hand causes you to sin, cut it off and throw it away! It's better for you to enter life maimed than keep both hands and go to hell, where the fire never goes out. And if it's your foot that leads you astray, chop it off! Better to enter life a cripple than keep both feet and have your whole body thrown into hell. And if it's your right eye, rip it out! Better to go one-eyed into the kingdom of God than keep both eyes and be cast into hell, where the devouring worm never dies and the fire is never put out.

"See that you never despise one of these little ones. I tell you they have their guardian angels in heaven who look continually on the face of my heavenly Father.

Make no mistake about it! Your Father in heaven does not want any of these little ones to be lost."

"If He's Not Against Us, He's for Us"

"Teacher," John told him, "we saw a man driving out devils in your name, and since he wasn't one of us we told him to stop."

"Don't stop him," said Jesus. "No one who performs a miracle in my name will be able in the same breath to speak evil of me. Whoever is not against us is for us."

"When a Brother Does Wrong"

Jesus taught them, "If a brother does wrong, go take the matter up with him strictly between yourselves. If he listens to you, you have won your brother over. If he will not listen, take one or two others with you so that 'all facts may be duly established on the evidence of two or three witnesses,' as the scripture says. If he refuses to listen to them, report the matter to the congregation. And if he will not listen even to the congregation, then consider him a pagan and a tax collector.

"I tell you this. Whatever you forbid on earth will be forbidden in heaven, and whatever you allow on earth will be allowed in heaven.

"Again, I tell you if two of you on earth agree about any request you have to make, that request will be granted by my Father in heaven. Wherever two or three come together in my name, I am there with them."

"Forgiveness Must Be Unlimited"

"If your brother does wrong, rebuke him, and if he repents, forgive him. Even if he wrongs you seven times in one day and comes back to you seven times, saying, 'I'm sorry,' you must forgive him.''

Peter came up to him and said, "Lord, suppose he keeps on wronging me? How many times do I have to keep forgiving him? Is seven the limit?"

"No," said Jesus, "not seven, but seventy times seven!"

The Parable of the Merciless Servant

"You must picture the kingdom of heaven like this:

"Once there was a king who decided to settle accounts with the men who served him. First there appeared before him a man whose debt ran into the millions. Since he had no means of paying, the king ordered him sold into slavery to meet the debt, with his wife, his children, and everything he had. The man fell prostrate at his master's feet. 'Be patient with me,' he pleaded, 'and I will pay in full.' The king felt so sorry for him that he let the man go and remitted the debt. But no sooner had the man gone out than he met a fellow servant who owed him only a hundred denarii. Grabbing him by the throat, he yelled, 'Pay me what you owe!' The man fell at his feet and begged him, 'Be patient with me, and I'll pay you back.' But he refused and had him jailed until he should pay the debt. The other servants were dismayed when they saw what had happened, and went to their master with the whole story. So he summoned the first servant. 'You scoundrel!' he said, 'I remitted your entire debt when you appealed to me. Shouldn't you have shown your fellow servant the same pity I showed you?' The king was so angry he condemned the man to torture until he should pay the debt in full.

"And that is how my Father in heaven will deal with you unless you each forgive your brother from your hearts."

Jesus Decides to Go to Jerusalem

As the Jewish Festival of Tabernacles was close at hand, Jesus' brothers counseled him, "You should leave Galilee and go to Judea so your disciples can see the great things you're doing. Surely nobody works in seclusion if he wants to be well known. If you're really doing such things as these, show yourself to the world." (Not even his brothers believed in him.)

Jesus told them, "The right time for me has not yet come, but any time is all right for you. The world can't hate you, but it hates me for exposing its wicked ways. You go on to the festival. I am not going up to this feast because the right time for me has not yet fully arrived." With this answer he stayed behind in Galilee.

Later, however, after his brothers had gone to the festival Jesus resolved to go to Jerusalem but without any publicity. He sent messengers ahead to make arrangements for him. They set out and came to a Samaritan village, but the villagers would not have him because he was making for Jerusalem.

When the disciples James and John were faced with such an inhospitable reception they asked Jesus, "Lord, do you want us to call down fire from heaven to burn them up?" But he turned and rebuked them, and they went on to another village.

V

In Jerusalem and Judea

Jesus at the Festival of Tabernacles

The Jews were looking for him at the festival and asking, "Where is he?" And there was much whispering about him among the people. Some said, "He is a good man," while others said, "No, he is leading the people astray." Yet nobody talked about him openly for fear of the Jews.

The festival was already half over when Jesus went to the Temple and began to teach. The Jews were astonished at his teaching.

"How," they said, "did this unschooled man come by such learning?"

Jesus replied, "The teaching I give is not my own. It comes from the one who sent me. If anybody's will

95

is to do *his* will he will know whether the teaching comes from God or is merely my own. A person who speaks on his own is out for self-glorification. But the person who seeks glory for the one who sent him can be relied on. There is nothing false in him.

"Moses gave you the Law, didn't he? Yet all of you break it. So why are you trying to kill me?"

"You're possessed!" the crowd answered. "Who wants to kill you?"

"I do one work on the Sabbath and you're all aghast. But think this over. Since Moses ordered you to circumcise your sons you circumcise a boy on the Sabbath. (Not that this practice originated with Moses. It was the patriarchs who started it.) Well then, if to avoid breaking this law of Moses you circumcise on the Sabbath, why are you angry with me because I made a man's whole body well on the Sabbath? Don't judge superficially but be just."

At this some of the people of Jerusalem began to say, "Isn't this the man they're seeking to put to death? Yet here he is, speaking in public, and they say nothing to him. Can it be the authorities really know this is the Messiah? On the other hand, we all know where this man comes from, but when the Messiah appears, nobody is to know where he comes from."

As Jesus taught in the Temple he spoke out, "You know me, and you know where I come from. But I have not come on my own. I was sent by the one who is true, and him you don't know. I know him because I come from him and he sent me."

At this they sought to seize him, but nobody laid a hand on him because his time had not yet come. Nevertheless among the people many believed in him. These said, "When the Messiah appears, is it likely he will work more wonders than this man has?"

The Pharisees overheard the crowd thus discussing him, so they and the chief priests sent Temple police to arrest him.

"I shall be with you a little longer," Jesus said. "Then I am going away to the one who sent me. You will look for me, but you won't find me. Where I am, you can't come."

The Jews asked each other, "Where does he plan on going that we won't be able to find him? Does he plan to go to the Jews dispersed among the Greek cities and teach the Greeks? What does he mean by saying, 'You will look for me, but you won't find me. Where I am, you can't come'?"

On the last and greatest day of the festival Jesus stood up and cried out, "If anyone is thirsty, let him come to me. Whoever believes in me, let him drink. As the scripture says, 'Out of his heart will flow streams of living water.'" (He was speaking of the Spirit which those who believed in him would receive later. At that time the Spirit had not yet been given because Jesus had not yet been raised to glory.)

Some of the people listening said, "This must be the prophet." Others said, "He is the Messiah." But still others said, "Surely everyone knows the Messiah won't come from Galilee! Doesn't scripture say the Messiah will be a descendant of David and will come from Bethlehem, David's town?" Thus divisions arose among the people. Some were for seizing him, but nobody laid hands on him.

The Temple police came back to the chief priests and Pharisees.

"Why haven't you brought him?" the latter demanded.

"No man ever talked like this man," they answered.

"Did he fool you too? Has a single one of the Pharisees or those in authority believed in him? As for this rabble who care nothing for the Law, a curse must be on them!"

One of the Pharisees, Nicodemus, the man who had once visited Jesus, intervened. "Does our Law allow us to pass judgment on a person without first giving him a hearing and learning the facts?"

"What! Are you a Galilean too? Study the scriptures and you will find no prophet is due to rise out of Galilee."

Jesus again addressed the people. "I am the light of the world. No follower of mine will wander in the dark. He will have the light of life."

"You are a witness in your own cause," the Pharisees told him. "Self-serving testimony is not valid."

"My testimony is valid even though I do bear witness about myself, because I know where I come from and where I am going. You know neither where I come from nor where I am going. You judge by worldly standards. I don't pass judgment on anyone, but if I were to judge, my judgment would be valid because it's not I alone who judge but I and the one who sent me. In your own Law it is written that if two witnesses agree, their testimony is valid. Here I am, a witness in my own cause, and my other witness is the Father who sent me."

"Where is your father?"

"You know neither me nor my Father. If you knew me you would know my Father as well."

These words were spoken by Jesus as he taught in the Temple in the treasury room. And nobody arrested him because his time had not yet come.

He said to them again, "I am going away. You will look for me, but you will die in your sin. Where I am going, you can't come."

"Will he kill himself?" asked the Jews. "Is that what he means when he says, 'Where I am going, you can't come'?"

He told them, "You belong to this world below. I belong to the world above. Your home is in this world. Mine is not. That is why I told you you would die in your sins. You will die in your sins unless you believe that I am."

"Who are you?" they asked him.

"I am from the beginning what I have told you. I have much to say about you, and in judgment. But the one who sent me speaks the truth, and I declare to the world only what I have heard from him."

They did not understand he was speaking to them about the Father. So he said to them, "When you have lifted up the Son of Man you will know that I am and that I do nothing on my own authority but speak only what the Father has taught me. And the one who sent me is with me. He has not left me alone, because I always do what pleases him."

Many Jews who heard Jesus say these things believed in him. Turning to those who had believed in him, Jesus said, "If you keep steadfast in my word, then you are really my disciples. You will know the truth, and the truth will set you free."

A retort came back. "We are descendants of Abraham and have never been slaves to anyone. So what do you mean, we will be 'set free'?"

"I am telling you the truth. Everybody who sins is a slave to sin. A slave has no permanent place in the household, but the son belongs there forever. So if the Son sets you free you will be free indeed.

"I know you are descendants of Abraham. Yet you are bent on killing me, because my word finds no welcome in you. I am revealing in speech what I saw in my Father's presence, while you are revealing in action what you heard from your father."

"Abraham is our father."

"If you were really Abraham's children you would do as Abraham did. But you seek to kill me, when all I have done is to tell you the truth as I heard it from God. That is not what Abraham did. You are imitating your own father."

"*We* were not conceived out of wedlock," they said. "God is our father and God alone."

"If God were your father you would love me, because God is the source of my being and I came from him. I did not come on my own. He sent me. Why don't you understand what I say? It is because you can't bear to hear my word. Your father is the devil, and your will is to carry out his desires. He was a murderer from the beginning and has nothing to do with the truth, because there is no truth in him. When he lies he is only doing what comes naturally, because he is a liar and the father of lies. But I speak the truth and that's why you don't believe me. Which of you can convict me of sin? If what I say is true, why don't you believe me? A child of God listens to God's words. The reason you don't listen to them is that you are not God's children."

"Aren't we right," the Jews answered, "in saying that you are a Samaritan and possessed?"

"I am not possessed. The truth is I am honoring my Father, but you dishonor me. I don't seek my own glory. There is one who does, and he will be the judge. I'm telling you the truth. Whoever keeps my word will never know what it is to die."

"Now we know for sure you are possessed. Abraham died and so did the prophets. Yet you say if anyone keeps your word he will never taste death. Do you claim to be greater than our father Abraham, who died? And the prophets, who died too? Who do you think you are, anyway?"

"If I make exalted claims for myself, such self-glorification is worthless. It is my Father who gives me glory, the very one you say is your God. But you have not really known him. I do. If I said I did not know him I would be a liar like you. But I do know him and keep his word. Your father Abraham was overjoyed that he would see my day. He saw it and was glad."

At this the Jews protested, "You can't yet be fifty. How could you possibly have known Abraham?"

"I'm telling you the truth. Before Abraham was born, I am."

They began picking up rocks to stone him, but Jesus was nowhere to be seen. He left the Temple secretly.

The Man Born Blind

As Jesus went on his way he saw a man blind from birth.

"Rabbi," his disciples asked him, "who sinned, this man or his parents? Why was he born blind?"

"It is not that this man or his parents sinned. God's works are going to be exemplified in him. We must do the works of the one who sent me while it is daylight. Night is coming when no one can work. As long as I am in the world I am the light of the world."

As he said this he spat on the ground, made some mud with the spittle, and spread it on the man's eyes. Then he told him, "Go wash in the pool of Siloam" (this word means "sent").

The man went off and washed his eyes, and when he returned he could see. His neighbors and those who had seen him begging said, "Isn't this the fellow who used to sit and beg?" Some said, "Yes, he's the one." Others said, "No, but he looks like him." He himself said, "I am the man."

"How were your eyes opened?" they asked him.

"The man named Jesus made some mud, smeared it on my eyes, and told me to go to Siloam and wash it off. I went and washed and received my sight."

"Where is he?"

"I don't know."

They brought the man before the Pharisees. Now it happened to be a Sabbath day when Jesus made the mud and opened his eyes.

The Pharisees put the same question to the man—how did he gain his sight? The man told them, "He put some mud on my eyes, then I washed, and now I can see."

Some of the Pharisees said, "The fellow who did this cannot be from God. He does not keep the Sabbath." But others said, "How could a sinner perform such miracles as this?" So their opinions were divided.

They turned to the man again and asked him, "What do you say about him? It was your eyes he opened."

"He is a prophet."

The Jews would not believe that the man had been blind and had gained his sight until they called his parents and questioned them. "Is this man your son? And do you say he was born blind? Then how come he can see now?"

"We know this is our son and that he was born

blind. But how it is he can see now, or who opened his eyes, we have no idea. Ask him. He's old enough to speak for himself."

His parents gave this answer because they were afraid of the Jews. The Jewish authorities had already agreed that anyone who acknowledged Jesus to be the Messiah was to be banned from the synagogue. This is why the parents said, "He's of age. Ask him."

So they summoned the man born blind again and told him, "Now before God, admit the truth. We know this Jesus is a sinner."

"Whether or not he's a sinner I don't know. But one thing I do know. Once I was blind and now I can see."

"What did he do to you? How did he open your eyes?"

"I've already told you, but you would not listen. Why do you want to hear it again? Do you want to become his disciples?"

Then they became abusive. "You are that man's disciple, but we are disciples of Moses. We know God spoke to Moses, but as for this fellow Jesus, we have no idea where he comes from."

"This is really fantastic! Here is a man who opened my eyes, and you say you have no idea where he comes from. Everybody knows God does not listen to sinners. He listens to people who worship him and do his will. To open the eyes of a man born blind, why it is unheard of since time began! If this man had not come from God he could not do anything."

At that they kicked him out of the synagogue. "Who are you to teach us lessons, you who were born and bred in sin?"

Jesus heard they had kicked him out. When he found him he asked him, "Do you believe in the Son of Man?"

"Tell me who he is, sir, so I can believe in him."

"You have already seen him. In fact he is speaking to you now."

"Lord, I believe!" the man said and fell on his knees in front of him.

"It is for judgment I came into this world," Jesus said, "—to give sight to the blind and to blind those with sight."

Some Pharisees nearby heard this and asked him, "Do you mean we are blind too?"

"If you were blind you would be guiltless. But because you say, 'We can see,' your guilt persists."

"I Am the Door of the Sheepfold"

"I'm telling you the truth. Whoever enters the sheepfold not by the door but by some other way is nothing but a thief and a bandit. The one who comes in by the door is the shepherd of the sheep. The doorkeeper opens the sheepfold for him. The sheep hear his voice, and he calls his own by name and leads them out. After bringing all his own sheep out he goes on ahead of them, and the sheep follow because they know his voice. They will not follow a stranger but will run from him, because they do not recognize the voice of strangers."

This was the figure Jesus employed with them, but they failed to comprehend his meaning. So he spoke again.

"I tell you I am the door of the sheepfold. All those who came before me are thieves and bandits, but the sheep paid them no heed. I am the door. If anyone comes into the fold through me he will be saved and will go in and out and find pasture. The thief comes only to steal, kill, and destroy. I have come to give life, and that in abundance."

"I Am the Good Shepherd"

"I am the good shepherd. The good shepherd is willing to die for the sheep. The hired man when he sees the wolf coming abandons the sheep and runs away, because he is no shepherd and the sheep are not his. Then the wolf harries the flock and scatters the sheep. The man runs away because he is only a hireling and doesn't care anything for the sheep.

"I am the good shepherd. I know my own sheep and my own know me, just as the Father knows me and I know the Father. And I am willing to die for them. There are other sheep of mine, not of this fold, whom I must bring in, and they too will listen to my voice. Then there will be one flock and one shepherd.

"The Father loves me because I am willing to lay down my life, to receive it back again. Nobody takes it from me. I give it up of my own free will. I have power to lay it down and power to take it back again. This is what my Father charged me to do."

These words caused another split among the Jews. Many of them said, "He's possessed! Raving mad! Why listen to him?" Others said, "Nobody possessed by a demon speaks like this. Could a demon open blind men's eyes?"

Jesus Resumes His Travels;
The Three Claimants to Discipleship

As they were going along the road a lawyer came up to him and said, "Teacher, I will follow you wherever you go."

Jesus told him, "Foxes have holes and birds have nests, but the Son of Man does not even have a place to lie down."

He told another to follow him, but the person replied, "Sir, let me go bury my father first."

"Leave the dead to bury their dead. You must go announce the kingdom of God."

Still another one said, "I will follow you, sir, but let me first say goodbye to my folks at home."

"Nobody who sets his hand to the plow and then keeps looking back is fit for the kingdom of God."

The Mission of the Seventy

After this Jesus appointed seventy messengers, paired them off, and sent them on ahead of him to visit every town and place along his route. These were the instructions he gave them.

"The harvest is great, but the workers are scarce. So pray the Lord of the harvest to send out more workers to harvest his crop.

"Be on your way and remember I am sending you out like lambs among wolves. Don't carry any wallet or pack, and travel barefoot. Don't stop to greet anyone on the road.

"Whenever you enter a house, let your first words be, 'Peace to this house!' If a child of peace lives there your blessing will rest on him; if not, it will come back to you. And stay in that same house, eating and drinking whatever they provide. The worker earns his keep. Don't move around from house to house.

"Whenever you enter a town and they make you welcome, eat what is set before you, heal the sick there, and say, 'The kingdom of God has come close to you.' But whenever you come into a town and they do not welcome you, go out in its streets and declare, 'Even the very dust of your town that sticks to our feet we wipe off to your shame. But remember this. The kingdom of God came near you!' I tell you it will be more tolerable for Sodom on the great day than for that town!"

Then he began to reproach the towns in which he had performed most of his miracles, because they did not repent.

"Woe to you, Chorazin! And you too, Bethsaida! If the miracles performed in you had been performed in Tyre and Sidon they would have repented long ago in sackcloth and ashes. Remember, then, it will be more tolerable for Tyre and Sidon on the day of judgment than for you.

"And as for you, Capernaum, will you be lifted to the skies? No! You will be plunged to the depths! If the miracles performed in you had been performed in Sodom, Sodom would be standing to this very day. I tell you it will be more tolerable for the land of Sodom on the day of judgment than for you.

"Whoever listens to you listens to me. Whoever rejects you rejects me. And whoever rejects me rejects the one who sent me."

The seventy returned jubilant. "In your name, Lord, even the demons obeyed us!"

He replied, "I saw Satan fall like lightning out of the sky. And now you see I have given you power to tread underfoot snakes and scorpions and all the forces of the enemy, and he will have no way at all to harm you. You should, however, be rejoicing not so much in the fact that the evil spirits obey you but in the fact that your names are written in heaven."

Jesus was filled with the joy of the Holy Spirit and exclaimed, "O Father, Lord of heaven and earth! Thank you for hiding these things from the wise and learned and revealing them to simple folk. Yes, Father, I am grateful such was your choice."

Turning to his disciples, he said, "Everything has been entrusted to me by my Father. And nobody knows who the Son is except the Father, or who the Father is except the Son and anyone to whom the Son chooses to reveal him."

Then he told his disciples in private, "How happy are the eyes that see what you are seeing and the ears that hear what you are hearing! I tell you many prophets and kings longed to see what you now see yet never saw it, and to hear what you hear but never heard it."

The Parable of the Good Samaritan

On one occasion a lawyer came forward to put Jesus to the test. "Teacher, what must I do to inherit eternal life?"

"What is written in the Law? What do you understand it to say?"

"Love the Lord your God with all your heart, with all your soul, with all your strength, and with all your mind, and your neighbor as yourself."

"That is the right answer. Do that and you will live."

The man, however, wanting to justify himself, proceeded to ask Jesus, "But who is my neighbor?"

This was Jesus' reply. "A fellow was traveling down to Jericho from Jerusalem and happened to fall in with bandits, who stripped him and beat him up and went off leaving him half dead. Now by chance a priest was going along the same way, but when he saw the poor man he skirted around him on the other side of the road. So too, a Levite when he came by and saw the man ignored him and went on past on the other side. But a Samaritan making the same journey came on the man, and when he saw him his heart was filled with pity. He went over and bandaged his wounds, bathing them with oil and wine. Then he lifted him up and set him on his own animal and brought him to an inn where he looked after him. The next day he took out two denarii and handed them to the innkeeper, saying, 'Take good care of him, and if you spend any more than this I will pay you back when I return.'

"Now which of these three, do you think, proved a neighbor to the man attacked by bandits?"

"The one who showed him kindness," the lawyer answered.

"You go, then, and do as he did."

Mary and Martha

As they went on their way Jesus came to a village where a woman named Martha made him welcome in her home. She had a sister named Mary who seated herself at the Lord's feet, listening to his teaching. Martha, however, was distracted by all the work she had to do in serving, so she came to him and complained.

"Lord, don't you care that my sister has left me to do all the work by myself? Tell her to come lend a hand."

"Martha, Martha, you're fretting and fussing over so many things, but only one thing is really necessary. Mary has chosen the good part, and it won't be taken away from her."

"Be Careful Your Light Isn't Darkness"

At another time Jesus said, "Your eye is the lamp of your body. If your eyes are sound you have light for your whole body, but if your eyes are bad your whole body is in darkness. So be careful the light in you is not darkness. If your light turns out to be darkness, how terribly dark it will be! But if your whole body is full of light, with no trace of darkness, then it will be bright all around, just as when a lamp shines on you."

"Guard Against Hypocrisy"

Meanwhile a throng of many thousands had collected, packed so close they were stepping on each other's toes. He began to speak first to his disciples.

"Be on your guard against the yeast of the Pharisees. I mean their hypocrisy. There is nothing covered up that won't be brought out in the open, nothing hidden that won't be disclosed, no secret that won't come to light. So you can be sure everything you have said in the dark will be heard in broad day, and what you have whispered behind closed doors will be shouted from the housetops."

The Parable of the Rich Fool

One fellow in the throng said to him, "Teacher, tell my brother to divide the family property with me."

"Man, who made me judge or arbitrator over your dispute?" he replied. Then he turned to the people.

"Be on your guard against greed in any form. A person's life is not to be gauged by the extent of his possessions." And he told them this parable.

"Once there was a rich man whose land produced great crops. He thought to himself, 'What shall I do? I don't have enough space to store all my crops. This is what I shall do. I shall tear down my barns and build bigger ones, and there I shall store up all my grain and other goods. Then I shall say to myself, "You've got plenty laid by now, enough for many years, so take life easy, eat, drink, and enjoy yourself!' ' But God said to him, 'You fool! This very night you must give up your life. And all these things you have got ready, who will own them now?'

"That is how it is with those who pile up wealth for themselves but stay paupers in God's sight."

"I Came to Set the World on Fire"

"I came to set the world on fire, and how I wish it were already kindled! I have a baptism to undergo, and how confined I am until the ordeal is over!

"Do you think I came to bring peace to the world? On the contrary, I came to bring division! From now on, a family of five will be divided three against two and two against three, father against son and son against father, mother against daughter and daughter against mother, and mother against her daughter-in-law and daughter-in-law against her mother-in-law. One will find his worst enemies under his own roof."

Reading the Signs of the Times; the Parable of the Barren Fig Tree

He also told the throngs, "When you see clouds forming in the west you say right off, 'It's going to rain,' and rain it does. And when the wind starts up from the south you say, 'There will be a heat wave,' and there is. You hypocrites! You know how to read the appearance of earth and sky. Why then can't you read the signs of this fateful time?

"And why can't you see for yourselves what is called for? If somebody sues you and takes you to court you do your best to settle with him quickly, before you get there. Otherwise, he will drag you before the judge, the judge will hand you over to the guard, and the guard will throw you in jail. And as you well know, once you are there you will never get out till you have paid the very last penny!"

Some people were present at the time who told Jesus about the Galilean rebels whose blood Pilate had mixed with their sacrifices.

"Do you think," he replied, "that because those Galileans suffered such a fate they were worse sinners than all other Galileans? I tell you they were not. But unless you repent you will all come to the same end.

"And what about the eighteen people crushed by the tower at Siloam? Do you imagine they were greater offenders than all the other inhabitants of Jerusalem? No, I tell you! But unless you repent you will all come to the same end."

Then Jesus told them this parable. "A man had a fig tree in his vineyard. He came looking for fruit on it but didn't find any. So he said to his gardener, 'Look here, for the last three years I have come looking for fruit on this fig tree and what have I found? Nothing! So cut it down. Why let it go on cluttering up the vineyard?' The gardener answered him, 'Let it alone, sir, this year while I dig around it and fertilize it. Then if it bears fruit next season, well and good, but if not, you can cut it down.'"

Another Sabbath Healing: The Crippled Woman

One Sabbath Jesus was teaching in a synagogue. A woman was there, possessed by an evil spirit that had crippled her for eighteen years. She was bent over and unable to stand up straight.

When Jesus saw her he called her and told her, "Woman, you are freed from your infirmity." Then he placed his hands on her, and at once she straightened up and praised God.

The synagogue official was indignant with Jesus for doing this on the Sabbath and told the congregation, "There are six workdays in the week. Come be healed on one of those days, not on the Sabbath!"

Jesus gave him this answer. "You hypocrites! Every one of you would untie his ox or donkey from the stall and lead it out to water on the Sabbath. This woman, by contrast, is a daughter of Abraham, and Satan has kept her tied up for eighteen long years! Shouldn't she be freed from her bonds on the Sabbath?"

At these words all his opponents were put to shame, while the people were delighted at the wonderful things he was doing.

Jesus at the Festival of Hanukkah

It was winter, and the festival of the Dedication was taking place at Jerusalem. Jesus was walking in the Temple precincts, in Solomon's cloister.

The Jews gathered around him and asked, "How long are you going to keep us in suspense? Tell us the plain truth. Are you the Messiah or not?"

"I have already told you, but you do not believe. The deeds I have done in my Father's name, they are my credentials. But you do not believe because you are not sheep of my flock. My sheep listen to my voice, I know them, and they follow me. I give them eternal life. They shall never perish, and nobody will snatch them away from me. My Father who has given them to me is greater than everyone, and nobody can snatch them out of his hands. The Father and I are one."

Once again the Jews picked up rocks to stone him. But Jesus asked them, "I have shown you many good works done by my Father's power. For which of these are you stoning me?"

"We are not stoning you for any of those deeds but for your blasphemy. You, a mere man, make yourself out to be God!"

"Is it not written in your own Law, 'I said, "You are gods" '? If, then, those people are called gods to whom the word of God was delivered (and scripture cannot be set aside), why do you charge me, whom the Father consecrated and sent into the world, with blasphemy because I said, 'I am God's son'? If I am not doing the works my Father would, then do not believe me, but if I am, then at least accept the evidence of the deeds themselves even though you do not believe me, so you can recognize that the Father is in me and I am in the Father."

At this they tried once more to arrest him, but he escaped their clutches.

VI

Into Perea and Back

Jesus Retires Into Perea, Territory of Herod Antipas

Jesus crossed the Jordan again and went to the place where John had been baptizing earlier and there remained. Crowds followed him there. "John," they said, "did not do any signs, but everything he said about this man was true." And many people there came to believe in him.

"Go in the Narrow Door"

He resumed his journey through towns and villages, teaching as he kept on his course toward Jerusalem.

"Sir," somebody asked him, "will only a few be saved?"

"Strive to get in by the narrow door. Many people, I tell you, will try to go in and not be able. Once the master of the house has gotten up and locked the door you will begin to arrive and pound on the door and say, 'Sir, let us in!' But his answer will be, 'I don't know where you come from!' Then you will say, 'We ate and drank at the same table with you, and you taught in our streets.' But he will repeat, 'I tell you I don't know where you come from. Get away from me, all you wrongdoers!'

"What wailing and gritting of teeth there will be when you see Abraham and Isaac and Jacob and all the prophets in the kingdom of God and you yourselves locked out! People will come from the east and the west, from the north and the south, and sit down for the feast in the kingdom of God. Yes, and some who are now last will be first, and some who are first will be last."

"A Prophet Must Die in Jerusalem"

At that time some Pharisees came up and told him, "You had better leave here and get on your way. Herod is out to kill you."

"Go tell that fox, 'Listen! It is unthinkable that a prophet should meet his death anywhere but Jerusalem. I must resume my course soon enough. But for the time being I cast out demons and perform cures. It is on the third day I finish my race.'

"O Jerusalem, Jerusalem! Always killing the prophets and stoning the messengers sent you! How often I would have gathered your children together like a hen collecting her chicks under her wings, but you would not let me. Look, your house is deserted and desolate! I tell you, you will not see me again until you say, 'God bless the one who comes in the name of the Lord.' "

At the Banquet of a Chief Pharisee; the Man with Dropsy

One Sabbath Jesus was invited to dine at the house of a leader who belonged to the party of the Pharisees, and they were watching him closely. A man showed up in front of him, suffering from dropsy.

"Is it legal to heal on the Sabbath or not?" Jesus asked the lawyers and Pharisees. But they kept their mouths shut.

He took the man and cured him and sent him on his way. Then he said to them, "If any of you had a donkey or an ox that had fallen in a well, would you hesitate an instant to pull it out on the Sabbath?"

They had no reply to this.

When he noticed how the guests were scrambling to get the seats of honor he told them a parable. "When anyone invites you to a wedding feast, don't grab one of the seats of honor. Somebody more eminent than you may have been invited, and the host will have to come tell you to give up your seat to him. Then think how ashamed you will be as you move down to the lowest place at the table. Instead, whenever you receive an invitation, go sit down in the lowest place, so that when your host arrives he'll say, 'Friend, come on up here.' Then all the other guests will see the esteem in which you're held. Remember, everybody who promotes himself will be humbled, and whoever humbles himself will be promoted."

Jesus addressed his host too. "Whenever you give a dinner or banquet, don't invite your friends, your brethren, your relatives, or your rich neighbors. They will invite you in return and thus repay your hospitality. Instead, when you give a party, ask the poor, the maimed, the crippled, and the blind, and you will find happiness. They have no way to repay you, but you will be paid back when the just rise from the dead."

The Cost of Discipleship

Great throngs accompanied Jesus, and he turned and told them, "Whoever comes to me cannot be my disciple unless he hates his own father and mother and spouse and children and brothers and sisters, yes, and even his own life. Nobody who does not carry his own cross and follow behind me can be my disciple.

"Would any one of you think of building a tower without first sitting down and counting the cost to see if he has enough money to finish the job? Otherwise, if he lays a foundation and then cannot complete it people watching his project will make fun of him. 'That fellow,' they will say, 'started to build and couldn't finish!'

"Or what king with ten thousand men will march off to do battle with another king who has twenty thousand, without first sitting down to decide whether he is strong enough to face such an enemy? If he concludes he can't, he sends an ambassador while the other is still a long way off, and asks for peace terms.

"So likewise none of you can be my disciple without renouncing everything he has."

The Parable of the Lost Sheep

The tax collectors and outcasts were all pressing in to listen to him. The Pharisees and the lawyers began muttering, "Look how this man welcomes sinners and even eats with them."

Jesus answered them with this parable. "Suppose

one of you has a hundred sheep and loses one of them. What would he do? He would leave the other ninety-nine out on the hillside and go looking for the stray until he finds it. Once he has found it he is so happy that he hoists it up on his shoulders, brings it home, and calls in his friends and neighbors, crying, 'Come on and celebrate with me! I have found my lost sheep!' He is more delighted over that one sheep than over the ninety-nine that never went astray. Just like this, I tell you, there will be more joy in heaven over one sinner who repents than over ninety-nine virtuous people who have no need to repent."

The Parables of the Lost Coin and
the Prodigal Son

"Or suppose a woman has ten drachmas and loses one of them. Doesn't she light a lamp and sweep the house and search every nook and cranny until she finds it? And when she has found it she calls her friends and neighbors together and says, 'Come celebrate with me! I have found the coin I lost!' In the same way, I tell you, there is joy among God's angels over one sinner who repents.

"Again, there was once a man who had two sons, and the younger said to his father, 'Father, give me my share of the inheritance.' So the man divided his property between them. A few days later the younger son converted his share into cash and took off for a distant land where he squandered it in reckless living.

"Just when he had spent it all a great famine swept that country, and he began to feel the pinch. So he went and hired himself out to one of the local citizens, who sent him into the fields to tend his hogs. He would gladly have filled his stomach with the pods the hogs ate, but nobody gave him anything.

"He finally came to his senses and asked himself, 'How many of my father's hired hands have food enough and to spare, and here I am starving to death! I shall get up and go to my father and say to him, "Father, I have sinned both against God and against you. I am no longer fit to be called your son. Just treat me like one of your hired men."' So he got up and set out for home.

"While he was still a long way off, his father saw him and his heart went out to him, and he ran and threw his arms around him and kissed him. 'Father,' the son started to say, 'I have sinned against heaven and against you. I am no longer worthy to be called your son.' But the father interrupted him. 'Quick!' he called to his servants, 'Bring my best robe and put it on him! Get a ring for his finger and shoes for his feet! Then go get the prize calf and slaughter it, and let's have a great feast! This my son was dead and has come back to life! He was lost and is found!' And the festivities began.

"Now the older son had been out working in the fields, and as he approached the house he heard the music and dancing. So he called one of the servants and asked what was going on. The servant replied, 'Your brother has come home, and your father is so glad to have him back safe and sound he has slaughtered the prize calf.'

"The older brother was so angry he refused to go in and join the celebration. His father came out and begged him to come on in, but he answered back to his father, 'You know how I have slaved for you all these years and never once disobeyed you, yet you have never given me so much as a goat for a feast with my friends. But up comes this son of yours after running through all your money with his whores, and what do you do? You kill the prize calf for him!'

" 'Son,' the father replied, 'you are always by my side, and everything I have is yours. How can we help but celebrate this happy day? Here your brother was dead and has come back to life, was lost and is found!' "

The Parables of the Shrewd Manager and of the Rich Man and Lazarus

Jesus also told his disciples, "There was a rich man who employed a manager, and accusations were brought to his attention that this man was wasting his property. So he called him in and said, 'What's this I hear about you? Turn in your accounts. You can't be manager here any longer.'

"The manager said to himself, 'What will become of me now that I am fired? I am not strong enough to dig ditches, and I am too proud to beg. I know what I will do. I will make sure I have a roof over my head after I'm out of this job!'

"So he summoned his master's debtors one by one. To the first one he said, 'How much do you owe my master?' The man answered, 'A thousand gallons of olive oil.' The manager said, 'Here is your account. Quick now, sit down and make it five hundred.' Then he said to another one, 'And how much do you owe?' The fellow replied, 'A thousand bushels of wheat.' The manager told him, 'Here, take your bill and make it eight hundred.' "

The Lord commended the dishonest manager for his prudence, because the children of this world are wiser in *their* day and age than the children of light. "I tell you, use your worldly wealth to win friends, so that when money is a thing of the past they will welcome you into the eternal home. The person who can be trusted in little things can be trusted in great ones too, but whoever is dishonest in small matters is likewise dishonest in big ones. So if you prove untrustworthy with the wealth of this world, who will trust you with the true wealth? And if you have been unfaithful with what belongs to somebody else, who will give you your own?"

When the Pharisees heard all this they made fun of Jesus, because they loved money. He told them, "You are the ones always at pains to make yourselves look right in people's eyes, but God sees through you! What people praise is detestable in God's sight.

"Once there was a rich man always dressed in purple and fine linen, who feasted sumptuously every day of the week. At his gate lay a poor man named Lazarus, covered with sores and begging to be given the scraps that fell from the rich man's table. Dogs would come up and lick his sores.

"One day the poor man died and was carried up by the angels to Abraham's side. The rich man died too and was buried. As he looked up from his torment in hell he saw Abraham far away and Lazarus by his side. He called out, 'Father Abraham! Please take pity on me and send Lazarus to dip his finger in some water and cool my tongue. I am in agony in this fire!'

"Abraham answered, 'My son, remember how you in your lifetime had all the good things and Lazarus all the bad? Now he has his consolation, and you are the one in agony. But besides, there is a great gulf fixed between us and you. Nobody who wants to reach you from our side can cross it, and nobody from your side can reach us.'

"The rich man replied, 'Then father, I beg you, send him back to my parents' house to warn my five brothers so they, at least, can avoid this place of torment.' But Abraham said, 'They have Moses and the prophets. Let them pay heed to them.'

" 'That is not enough, father Abraham,' the rich man said, 'but if somebody from the dead goes to them they will repent.' Abraham answered, 'If they won't listen to Moses and the prophets they won't be convinced even if someone were to rise from the dead.' "

"We Have Only Done Our Duty"

"Suppose one of you has a servant plowing or looking after sheep. When he comes in from the fields, would you the master tell him, 'Come right on in and sit down at the table'? Of course not. Instead, you would say to him, 'Fix my supper, then buckle your belt and wait table for me until I'm through eating. Afterwards, you can have your supper.' And would you thank him just for obeying orders?

"It should be the same with you. When you have done everything you were ordered to, you ought to say, 'We don't deserve any credit. We are servants and have only done our duty.' "

Lazarus Raised From the Dead

A man had fallen ill, namely Lazarus of Bethany— the village of Mary and her sister Martha. (This Mary was the one who later anointed the Lord with ointment and wiped his feet with her hair. It was her brother Lazarus who was sick.)

The sisters sent a message to Jesus to let him know his dear friend was ill. When Jesus heard it he said, "This sickness won't be fatal. It was destined for the glory of God, to bring glory to the Son of God."

Jesus loved Martha and her sister and Lazarus. After receiving the news of Lazarus' illness he remained where he was for two more days. Then he told his disciples, "Let's go back into Judea."

"Rabbi," the disciples objected, "it has been almost no time since the Jews there were trying to stone you. Surely you are not going back there?"

"The day brings twelve hours of light, doesn't it? If anybody walks in the day he won't stumble, because he has the light of the world to guide him. But if he walks in the night he will, because the light is not in him." Then he added, "Our friend Lazarus has fallen asleep, but I go to wake him up."

"Master, if he has gone to sleep that means he will recover."

Jesus, however, was talking about death, but they thought he meant ordinary restful sleep. Then Jesus made it plain.

"Lazarus is dead. For your sake I am glad I was not there, so you will believe. But come on, let's go to him."

Thomas, called "the Twin," said to his fellow disciples, "Let's all go along with our Master, to die with him!"

When Jesus arrived he found Lazarus had already been in the tomb four days. Bethany was not far from Jerusalem, about two miles, and many of the Jews had come to offer their condolences to Martha and Mary.

When Martha heard Jesus was coming she went out to meet him, leaving Mary at home.

"Lord," she said, "if you had been here my brother would still be alive. And I know that even now whatever you ask of God he will give you."

"Your brother will rise again," Jesus told her.

"Yes, I know he will rise in the resurrection of the last day."

"I am the resurrection and the life. Whoever believes in me, even though he dies, will live. And whoever is alive and believes in me will never die. Do you believe this?"

"Yes, Lord, I do believe you are the Messiah, the Son of God, the one coming into the world."

Then she went back to call her sister Mary and, taking her aside, told her, "The teacher is here and asking for you." When Mary heard this she got up quickly and went to him.

Now Jesus was still outside the village, where Martha had met him. When the Jews who were in the house consoling Mary saw her get up so quickly and hurry out, they followed her, supposing she was going to the tomb to wail there.

Mary, nearing the spot where Jesus had stopped, caught sight of him and fell at his feet. "Lord, if only you had been here my brother would still be alive!"

When Jesus saw her crying and the Jews who accompanied her wailing too, he was deeply aroused and disturbed.

"Where have you put him?" he asked.

"Come see, Lord," they said.

Jesus broke into tears. The Jews remarked, "Look how much he loved him!" But some said, "Couldn't this fellow who opened the blind man's eyes have done something to keep Lazarus from dying?"

Jesus, again deeply aroused, reached the tomb. It was a cave, the mouth of which had been sealed with a stone.

"Take the stone away!" Jesus ordered.

Martha the dead man's sister spoke up. "Lord, by this time there will be quite a stench. He has been dead four days."

Jesus turned to her. "Didn't I tell you if you would believe you would see the glory of God?" So they removed the stone.

Jesus looked upward. "I thank you, Father, that you have heard me. I know you always hear me, but I have said this for the sake of the people standing here, so they may believe you sent me." Then he raised his voice and called, "Lazarus! Come out!"

The dead man came out, his hands and feet wrapped in linen bands and his face covered with a cloth.

"Unwrap those bands," Jesus told them, "and let him go."

Many of the Jews—those who had come to visit Mary and had seen what Jesus did—believed in him, but others went off to the Pharisees and reported what he had done.

The chief priests and the Pharisees convened a meeting of the Council, and the question was put, "What action should we take? This man is performing many wonders. If we let him go on like this, everybody will believe in him. Then the Romans will come and destroy both our Temple and our nation."

One of them—Caiaphas—who was high priest that year spoke out. "Ignorant men, use your heads! Can't you see it is more expedient that one man should die for the people than that the whole nation be wiped out?" (Actually he said this, not of his own accord but as high priest at the time. He was prophesying that Jesus would die for the nation, and not for it alone but to bring all together the children of God scattered abroad.)

So from that day on they plotted his death. As a

result Jesus no longer went about publicly in Judea but left for the area bordering the desert, where he stayed with his disciples in a town called Ephraim.

VII

The Final Pilgrimage

**Jesus Sets Out to Begin His Last Journey to
Jerusalem; the Ten Lepers**

With the approach of the Jewish Passover many
people were going up from the country to Jerusalem to
purify themselves before the festival. Jesus, to join the
pilgrimage from Galilee to Jerusalem, was passing
along the border of Samaria.

As he was entering a village he was met by ten
people with leprosy. They stood at a distance and called
out to him, "Jesus! Master! Take pity on us!"

Seeing them, he replied, "Go show yourselves to
the priests." And while they were on their way they were
made clean.

One of them, realizing he was healed, turned back,

praising God loudly. And prostrating himself at Jesus' feet, he thanked him. The man was a Samaritan.

At this Jesus said, "Weren't there ten made clean? Where are the other nine? Is this foreigner the only one found to come back and give praise to God?" And to the man he said, "Get up and go on your way. Your faith has made you well."

The Question About the Coming of the Kingdom of God

On another occasion he was asked by the Pharisees when the kingdom of God would come.

"The coming of the kingdom of God," he answered, "won't be announced by visible signs. Don't expect somebody to shout, 'Look! Here it is!' or 'There it is!', because in fact the kingdom of God is in your midst."

The Parable of the Widow and the Judge

He told his disciples a parable to show them they should keep on praying and never lose heart.

"In a certain town there was a judge who feared neither God nor public opinion. In the same town there was a widow who kept coming before him demanding justice, 'Help me against my opponent!' For a while he refused, but in the end he said to himself, 'True, I'm not afraid of either God or public opinion, but this widow is such a nuisance that either I must right her wrong or she'll keep on coming until she wears me out!' "

The Lord continued, "Now if that's how it is with an unjust judge, won't God vindicate his chosen ones who cry out to him day and night? Will he be slow to help them? I tell you he will vindicate them swiftly! But when the Son of Man comes, will he find faith on earth?"

The Parable of the Pharisee and the Publican

He also told this parable aimed at those who were confident of their own goodness and who looked down on others.

"Two men went up to the Temple to pray, one a Pharisee and the other a tax collector. The Pharisee stood up and prayed, 'I thank you, God, that I'm not like the rest of mankind, greedy, dishonest, immoral, or for that matter like this tax collector. I fast twice a week. I pay tithes on everything I get.' But the tax collector kept way toward the back and wouldn't even raise his eyes to heaven but beat on his breast, crying, 'O God, take pity on me a sinner!'

"It was this one, I tell you, rather than the other, who went home with his sins forgiven. Everyone who promotes himself will be humbled, but whoever humbles himself will be promoted."

About Divorce

Leaving Galilee, Jesus arrived in the vicinity of Judea on the far side of the Jordan River. Again great crowds surrounded him and trailed him. He healed them there and continued his usual practice of teaching.

Some Pharisees came up to test him. "Is it legal for a man to divorce his wife?" they asked.

"Haven't you read that from the beginning the Creator made them male and female and for this reason a man will leave his father and mother and unite with his wife and the two will become one? It follows that they are no longer two individuals, but one. What God, then, has joined together, man must not separate."

"Then why did Moses lay it down that a man could give his wife a notice of divorce and send her away?"

"It is because you were so callous that Moses allowed you to divorce your wives, but it was not that way from the beginning."

When they were indoors again, the disciples questioned him about this. He told them, "Whoever divorces his wife and marries another woman commits adultery against his wife. So too, the woman who leaves her husband and marries another man commits adultery, and anybody who marries a divorced woman commits adultery."

"If this is how a man stands with his wife," the disciples reacted, "it is better not to marry."

"That is a counsel not everyone can accept, but only those for whom God has appointed it. While some are incapable of marriage because they were born so or were made so by men, there are others who have renounced marriage for the sake of the kingdom of heaven. Let those accept it who can."

"Let the Little Children Come!"

People were bringing children and even infants to Jesus to have him put his hands on them and pray, but the disciples scolded them for it.

Jesus was indignant at this. Calling the children to him, he told his disciples, "Let the little ones come to me! Don't stop them. The kingdom of God belongs to such as these. Believe me, whoever does not accept the kingdom of God like a child will never get into it."

And he took them in his arms and, laying his hands on them, blessed them.

The Rich Young Ruler

Jesus was starting out on his way again when a man of the ruling class ran up and, kneeling in front of him, asked, "Good Teacher, what must I do to win eternal life?"

"Why do you call me good? Nobody is good but God alone. If you want to enter life, you know the commandments: Do not murder. Do not commit adultery. Do not steal. Do not lie. Do not cheat. Honor your father and mother. And love your neighbor as yourself."

"Teacher," the young man replied, "I have kept all these since I was a boy."

With love Jesus looked him straight in the eye and said, "There is one thing you still lack. Go sell everything you've got and give the money to the poor, and you will have riches in heaven. Then come follow me."

At these words the young man's face fell and he went away sad, because he was very rich. Jesus looked around at his disciples and sighed, "How hard it will be for rich people to enter the kingdom of God!"

The disciples were amazed to hear this, but Jesus insisted, "My children, how hard it is to get into the kingdom of God! It's easier for a camel to go through the eye of a needle than for a rich person to enter the kingdom of God."

They were more astonished than ever. "Then who can be saved?" they asked.

Jesus looked at them and replied, "With human beings this is impossible, but not with God. All things are possible with God."

"Look," Peter spoke up, "we have left everything and followed you."

"Yes," Jesus said, "but I tell you there's not a one who has given up field or home, brother or sister, mother or father, spouse or child for my sake and that of the good news, who won't receive a hundred times as much even in this age—homes, fields, brothers, sisters, mothers, children—together with persecutions, and in the age to come, eternal life. And in that new world when the Son of Man is seated on his throne in glory you my followers will have thrones of your own, to govern the twelve tribes of Israel. But many who are first will be last, and the last first."

The Parable of the Workers in the Vineyard

"The kingdom of heaven is like this. There was once a landowner who went out early in the morning to hire people to work in his vineyard. After agreeing to pay them the usual day's wage he sent them off to the vineyard to work.

"Going out again between about eight and nine o'clock, he saw some more standing idle in the marketplace, so he told them, 'Go on into the vineyard and join the others, and I'll pay you a fair wage.' So off they went.

"He went out again before noon and then about two or three o'clock and made the same arrangements as before. An hour before sunset he went back to the marketplace and found another group standing around and asked them, 'Why are you hanging around here all day with nothing to do?' 'Because nobody has hired us,' they replied. So he told them, 'You go on and work in the vineyard too.'

"At nightfall the lord of the vineyard instructed his foreman, 'Call the workers and pay them their wages, starting with those who were hired last and ending with the first.' The ones who were hired an hour before sunset came forward and each received a full day's wage.

"Now when it came the turn of those who were hired first they expected something extra, but each received the same as the others. As they took it they grumbled at the owner, 'These Johnny-come-latelies did only an hour's work, and you have treated them the same as us who have sweated the whole day long in the blazing sun!'

"Turning to one of them, the owner replied, 'Friend, I'm not being unfair to you. You agreed to do a day's work for this wage, didn't you? So take what's yours and go. I choose to give this last one the same as you. Can't I do as I please with what's mine? Or do you begrudge my generosity?' "

Jesus Again Forecasts His Death and Resurrection

They were now on the road going up to Jerusalem, with Jesus striding along in the lead. The disciples were filled with amazement, and those following behind were just plain scared. Taking the twelve aside as they walked along, Jesus began to tell them what was to happen to him.

"Listen! We are now going up to Jerusalem where everything predicted by the prophets about the Son of Man will come true. He will be handed over to the chief priests and the lawyers. They will condemn him to death and turn him over to the Gentiles, who will make fun of him, insult him, and spit on him. Then they will whip him and kill him, and on the third day he will rise again."

They, however, understood nothing of all this. They were bewildered by what he said, because its significance was hidden from them.

The Selfish Ambition of James and John

James and John the sons of Zebedee approached Jesus.

"Teacher, we want you to do us a favor."

"What is it you want?"

"Give us the right to sit next to you in your glory, one at your right hand and the other at your left."

"You don't know what you're asking. Can you drink the cup I must drink, or undergo the same baptism I do?"

"We can."

"It's true all right. You will share my cup. And the baptism I undergo, you will undergo. But to sit at my right hand or at my left is not mine to grant. These places belong to those for whom my Father has prepared them."

When word of this got back to the other ten they were indignant with James and John. But Jesus called them all together.

"You know how those appointed to rule the Gentiles lord it over them and how their great men make them feel the weight of authority. But that's not how it should be with you. Whoever wants to be great among you must be your servant, and whoever wants to be first among you must be the slave of everybody, like the Son of Man. He didn't come to be served but to serve, and to give his life as a ransom for many."

Bar-Timaeus the Blind Beggar

They reached Jericho. As they were approaching the city, followed by a large crowd, they passed a blind beggar named Bar-Timaeus ("son of Timaeus") sitting by the roadside. Hearing the crowd going by, he asked what was happening and was told, "Jesus of Nazareth is passing through."

"Jesus!" he began to shout, "Son of David! Take pity on me!"

Those in front told him to shut up and keep quiet, but he just shouted ever louder, "Son of David! Take pity on me!"

Jesus stopped and ordered them to call the man to him. So they called the blind man. "Cheer up! Get on your feet. He's calling you."

At that he threw off his coat, jumped up, and came to Jesus.

"What do you want from me?" Jesus asked him.

"Master, I want to see again."

Jesus felt sorry for him and touched his eyes. "Be on your way. Your faith has made you well."

Instantly the man recovered his sight, and he followed Jesus down the road, praising God. And when the crowd saw it they all joined in too.

Zacchaeus the Tax Collector

While Jesus was on his way through Jericho a rich man named Zacchaeus, the chief tax collector, was trying to see what he looked like, but being a little man was unable even to catch a glimpse of him because of the crowd. So he ran on ahead and climbed up a sycamore tree in order to get a view, since Jesus was to pass that way.

Jesus when he reached the spot glanced up and said, "Zacchaeus, hurry and come on down. I must stay at your house today."

Overjoyed, Zacchaeus scrambled down and welcomed him into his home. A murmur of disapproval ran through the crowd. "He has gone in to be the guest of a sinner!"

Zacchaeus drew himself up and addressed Jesus. "Right here and now, sir, I donate half of all my wealth to the poor, and if I have ever cheated anybody I stand ready to pay him back four times over."

"See!" Jesus said, "This man is a son of Abraham too! So salvation has come to this house today, because the Son of Man came to seek and to save what was lost."

The Parable of the Money in Trust

Jesus went on to tell those present the following parable, because he was close to Jerusalem and they supposed the kingdom of God was to appear at any moment.

"A nobleman went abroad to be appointed king and then return. But before he left he called ten of his servants and entrusted them with his property, giving each one a bag of money. 'Carry on trade with these till I come back,' he told them. Then he left.

"The first one went off at once and invested the money in trade and made ten more bags. Likewise, the second servant made five bags. But another one went off and dug a hole in the ground and buried his master's money.

"Now the nobleman's fellow citizens hated him and sent after him a delegation to block his appointment. Nevertheless after a long time he returned as king and summoned the servants to whom he had given the money, to learn how much profit they had made and to settle accounts with them.

"The first came forward. 'Master,' he said, 'your money has made ten times more.' 'Well done!' his master praised him. 'You are a good and faithful servant! Since you have proved trustworthy with very little, I will make you manager of much. You shall govern ten cities! Come share your master's joy!'

"Then the second came up and said, 'Master, your one bag has made five bags.' 'Well done!' the master said again, 'my good and faithful servant! Having proved trustworthy over little, you shall be manager over much. I will put you in charge of five cities. Come share your master's delight!'

"Then the other servant came. 'Master,' he said, 'here is your money all safely tied up in a handkerchief. I knew you to be a hard man, drawing out what you never put in, harvesting where you never planted, and gathering where you never scattered. I was afraid of you so I went and hid your money in the ground. Here, you can have back what is yours.'

" 'You lazy rascal!' his master exclaimed. 'Your very own words condemn you. You knew I was a hard man, drawing out what I never put in, harvesting where I never planted, and gathering where I never scattered. Then why didn't you at least put my money on deposit so that on my return I could have reclaimed it with interest?'

"Turning to his attendants, he said, 'Take the bag away from him and give it to the one with ten.' 'But sir,' they said, 'he already has ten bags!'

"The master went on, 'I tell you, to everyone who has something even more will be given, until he has enough and to spare, but from the one who is lacking, even the little he has will be taken away. Now throw that worthless servant out in the dark—the place of wailing and gritting of teeth. And as for these enemies of mine who didn't want me to be their king, bring them here and execute them in my presence!' "

Having finished the parable, Jesus again took the lead and began the ascent to Jerusalem.

VIII

Jerusalem! Jerusalem!

Anointed as King, But in Order to Die

The Jewish Passover was now at hand, and many people came up from the country to Jerusalem to perform the ceremony of purification before the festival. They were on the lookout for Jesus, and among the gatherings in the Temple there was much speculation whether he would show up at the festival or not. The chief priests and the Pharisees had given orders that anybody who knew his whereabouts should report it so they could arrest him.

Six days before the Passover Jesus reached Bethany where Lazarus lived—the man he had raised from the dead. While Jesus was there a supper was given in his honor at the house of Simon the Leper. Martha helped serve it, and Lazarus was one of the guests at the table.

During the meal Mary came up to Jesus with an alabaster flask of very expensive perfume—genuine nard—a whole pint of it. She opened it and anointed him with it, and poured some over his feet and wiped them with her hair. The whole house was filled with its fragrance.

Some of the disciples were indignant at her action. Judas Iscariot—the disciple who was to betray him—asked, "Why this waste? That jar of perfume could have been sold for more than three hundred denarii and the proceeds given to the poor!" (He said this, not because he cared for the poor but because he was a thief. He used to pilfer the common purse, which was in his charge.) So they took her to task.

"Leave her alone!" Jesus said. "Let her keep it for the day I am buried. Why should you make her unhappy? This is a beautiful thing she has done for me. The poor you always have with you, so you can do good for them anytime you please. But you will not always have me. She has done what she could, given my body the last rites in advance, prepared me for burial. Indeed, I tell you wherever the good news is proclaimed, the world over, this deed of hers will be told in her memory."

When the great crowd of Jews learned that Jesus was at Bethany they came to see not only him but also Lazarus whom he had raised from the dead. The chief priests then resolved to do away with Lazarus as well, because many Jews were going over to Jesus and believing in him on account of Lazarus.

The Triumphal Entry

The next day as Jesus and his disciples were approaching Jerusalem and came to Bethphage by the Mount of Olives he sent two of them off with these instructions.

"Go into the village over there, and just as you enter you will find a colt tied up that has never been ridden. Untie it and bring it here. If anybody asks you why you're doing that, say, 'The Master needs it and will send it back immediately.' "

So they went off and, following his instructions, found the colt standing in the street, tied to a door.

As they were untying it some bystanders asked, "What do you think you're doing, untying that colt?"

"The Master needs it," they replied and met no further objection.

They brought the young donkey to Jesus and threw their cloaks over its back, and he mounted. This was in fulfillment of the prophecy that says

"Tell the daughter of Zion,
'Here is your king,
Coming to you in gentleness,
Riding on a beast of burden,
Riding on the colt of a donkey.' "

His disciples did not understand this at the time, but after Jesus had been raised to glory they remembered that this had been written about him and had come true.

Now the people who had been present when Jesus called Lazarus from the tomb and raised him back to life had spread the word of it. Thus a tremendous throng of pilgrims who had come to the festival, on learning that Jesus was on his way into the city, gathered palm branches and went out to meet him.

Many of them spread their cloaks on the road in front of him, and others the branches they had cut. And as Jesus' party approached the descent from the Mount of Olives, all of them, both in front and behind, began to shout.

"Hosanna! God bless the one who comes in the name of the Lord! Hail, the Son of David! Hail, the coming kingdom of our father David! God bless the King of Israel! Peace in heaven and glory in the highest! Hosanna in the highest!"

As Jesus was thus being ushered into Jerusalem the Pharisees said to each other, "Look how all our efforts have come to nothing. Why, the whole world has gone running after him!"

Some of them in the crowd told Jesus, "Teacher! Reprimand your disciples!"

"I tell you," Jesus responded, "if they kept quiet the rocks themselves would shout!"

When he came in view of the city he cried over it, "If only you knew, even today, the way that leads to peace! But you can't see it. And the days are coming when your enemies will surround and besiege you, hemming you in on every side. They will bring you crashing down, you and the people within your walls. Not a single stone will they leave on top of another, all because you failed to recognize God's visit when it came."

As he entered Jerusalem the whole city was thrown into an uproar. "Who is it?" people asked excitedly, and the crowd answered back, "It's the prophet, Jesus from Nazareth of Galilee!"

He went to the Temple and looked around at everything. And the blind and the lame came to him there, and he healed them.

The chief priests and the lawyers, having seen the wonderful things he was doing and heard the boys shouting in the Temple, "Hosanna to the Son of David!" were filled with indignation and marched up to Jesus.

"Do you hear what they're yelling?" they demanded.

"Yes, I do," Jesus replied. "Haven't you ever read the scripture, 'From the mouths of children and babies you have drawn perfect praise'?"

With that he left them and since it was already late in the day went out to Bethany with the twelve, to spend the night there.

The Barren Fig Tree: The Parable Acted Out

The following morning on their way back to the city Jesus was hungry. Seeing off by the roadside a fig tree in leaf, he went to see if he could find anything on it. But reaching it he found nothing but leaves. It was not the season for figs. His disciples heard him say to the tree, "May nobody ever again eat fruit from you!"

The Clearing of the Temple

They arrived at Jerusalem and he entered the Temple. There he found the money-changers and the people who were selling cattle, sheep, and pigeons for sacrifice doing a brisk business. Making a whip of cords, he began driving them all out, both sellers and buyers, together with the sheep and cattle. He upset the tables of the money-changers, scattering their coins. Then he turned on the pigeon vendors, knocking over their stools.

"Take these things away!" he cried, "You will not

make my Father's house a house of trade!" And he would allow no one to use the Temple court as a thoroughfare for carrying goods.

Then he taught them. "Scripture says, 'My house shall be a house of prayer for all the nations.' But you have turned it into a bandits' hideaway!"

(His disciples recalled a scripture: "Zeal for your house will consume me like fire.")

"What sign can you show us for your authority to do this?" the Jews demanded.

"Destroy this sanctuary, and in three days I will raise it up."

They were astounded. "It has taken forty-six years to build this sanctuary, and you are going to build it back again in three days?"

But the sanctuary Jesus spoke of was his body. After he was raised from the dead his disciples remembered he had said this, and they believed the scripture and his word.

The chief priests, the lawyers, and the leaders of the people heard what he had done and sought a way to destroy him, because they were afraid of him. But they found themselves helpless, because the people all hung on his words.

Faith to Move Mountains

Every day Jesus could be found teaching in the Temple, but at dark when the people all went home he left the city and spent the night on the Mount of Olives. And early in the morning the people would crowd into the Temple to listen to him.

That next morning as Jesus and his disciples were on their way into the city they passed the fig tree and noticed that it had withered from the roots up. Peter, recalling what had happened, said to Jesus, "Look, Teacher! The fig tree you cursed has died!"

The disciples were astounded. "How could it have dried up so quickly?"

"Have faith in God," Jesus answered them. "Believe me, if you have faith, then causing a fig tree to wither is nothing compared with what you will be able to do. You can say to this hill, 'Get up and throw yourself in the sea!' and if you harbor no doubt in your heart but believe that what you say will happen, it will be done for you. So I tell you, whatever you ask in prayer, believe you have received it, and you will. But whenever you stand praying, always remember this. If you've got a grudge against anybody, forgive him, so that your Father in heaven may also forgive you the wrongs you've done."

The Woman Caught in Adultery

Early in the morning Jesus arrived again at the Temple and all the people collected around him. Having taken his seat, he was engaged in teaching them when the lawyers and Pharisees brought in a woman who had been caught in adultery.

Making her stand out in the middle, they said to him, "Teacher, this woman has been caught in the very act of adultery. Now in the Law Moses laid down the commandment that such women must be stoned to death. What do you say about it?"

They said this to trap him, so they could come up with some charge to bring against him.

Jesus bent down and wrote with his finger in the dirt. When they persisted in demanding an answer he stood up straight and replied, "Let the one among you who is completely innocent of sin be the first to throw a rock at her." Then once again he bent over and wrote with his finger on the ground.

One by one, starting with the elders, they began to melt away. Finally there was nobody left but Jesus and the woman standing in front of him.

Jesus straightened up again. "Where are they, woman? Has nobody sentenced you?"

"Nobody, sir."

"Well then, I don't sentence you either. Go on your way and don't sin again."

The Sanhedrin Challenges Jesus' Authority

As Jesus was walking in the Temple court the chief priests, the lawyers, and the elders of the people came up to him and demanded, "By what authority do you take these actions of yours? Who gave you the right to do what you are doing?"

"Let me put you a question, and if you give me an answer then I will inform you by what authority I act. Tell me, John's right to baptize, did it come from God or from man?"

This set them to arguing among themselves. "If we say, 'From God,' he will ask, 'Then why didn't you believe him?' But if we say, 'From man,' the people will stone us, because they are all convinced John was a real prophet."

At last they replied, "We don't know."

"Well then," said Jesus, "neither will I tell you by what authority I act."

The Parable of the Two Sons

He asked them what they thought about this.

"A man had two sons. He went to the first and said, 'Son, go work in the vineyard today.' 'I will, sir' the boy replied but never went. The father came to the second and made the same request. This one said no, but later changed his mind and went.

"Now which of the two did what his father wanted?"

"The second one," they answered.

"I'm telling you the truth. The tax collectors and prostitutes are crowding into the kingdom of God ahead of you. When John came to show you the right way to live, you didn't believe him, but the tax collectors and the prostitutes did. And even after you had seen that you didn't change your minds and believe him."

The Parable of the Bad Tenants

He went on to tell them another parable.

"A man planted a vineyard and enclosed it with a hedge, dug a pit for the winepress, and built a tower. Then he leased the vineyard out to tenants and went abroad for a long stay.

"When it came the season for fruit he sent a servant to the tenants to collect his share of the produce. They grabbed him, beat him up, and sent him away empty-handed.

"The landlord then sent a second servant. Him they also beat over the head, treated outrageously, and sent back without a thing. A third was sent, and they killed him. And so it was with many others, some beaten, some killed, some stoned.

"The man still had one more—a beloved son. Finally as a last resort, he sent him. 'Surely they will respect my son!' he thought. But when the tenants saw him they said to each other, 'This is the heir. Come on, let's kill him, and then the property will be ours.' So they seized him and killed him and threw his corpse out of the vineyard.

"Now when the owner of the vineyard comes, what will he do? He will destroy those bad tenants and turn the vineyard over to others who will pay him the fruit in season.

"So I tell you the kingdom of God will be taken away from you and given to a nation who will produce the fruits of it!"

"God forbid!" they cried.

Jesus looked straight at them and replied, "Then what does this mean written in the scriptures?

'The very block the builders rejected
has become the cornerstone.
This was the Lord's doing,
and how wonderful it is!'

Anyone who stumbles on that block will be dashed to pieces, and if it falls on a man it will crush him."

The chief priests, the Pharisees, and the lawyers, seeing that these parables were aimed at them, would have seized Jesus then and there but did not dare for fear of the crowds, who took him for a prophet. So they left him and went away.

The Parable of the Invitations

Somebody among those present, after hearing all this, exclaimed to Jesus, "How happy the one who will sit down to feast in the kingdom of God!" But Jesus responded to him with these parables.

"The kingdom of heaven is like this. Once a king was giving a wedding party for his son and had sent out many invitations. When the banquet was ready he sent his servants to summon the guests, but they wouldn't come. So he sent still others, instructing them to tell the guests, 'See here! I've completed all the preparations for my banquet. My steers and prize calves have been butchered, and everything is ready. So come on to the wedding feast.' But they ignored the message.

"Some made excuses. The first said, 'I've bought some land and have to go out and look it over. Please accept my regrets.' Another said, 'I've just bought five yoke of oxen and am on my way to try them out. Please excuse me.' Still another said, 'I've just got married, so I can't come.' The rest grabbed the servants, abused them, and killed them.

"The king was furious. He sent his troops to make an end of those murderers and burn their city to the ground. Then he told his servants, 'The wedding feast is ready, but those who were invited didn't deserve it. Go out right now into the streets and alleys of the city and bring in the poor, the crippled, the blind, and the lame.'

"A servant brought back the reply, 'Sir, your orders have been carried out, and there's still room to spare.' So he told the servant, 'Then go out into the highways and the hedges and pull in everybody you can find. I want my house to be full. And I tell you, not one of those who were invited shall taste my banquet!' "

The Parable of the Wedding Clothes

"The servants went out into the streets and invited everyone they could find, good and bad alike. And the wedding hall was packed with guests.

"When the king came in to look at them he observed one man not dressed up for a wedding. 'Friend,' he asked him, 'how did you get in here without proper attire?' But the fellow stood there speechless.

"The king then ordered his attendants, 'Tie that man up hand and foot and throw him out in the dark— the place of wailing and gritting of teeth.' "

And Jesus concluded, "Although many are invited, few are chosen."

"Is It Right to Pay Taxes to Caesar?"

The Pharisees went and agreed on a scheme to trap Jesus into saying something for which he could be prosecuted before the Governor. The chief priests and the lawyers, who were keeping a watch on Jesus, sent some of these as spies along with certain Herodians. Pretending to be sincere, they came up to him.

"Teacher, it is obvious that you are a fearless and forthright man, that you would proclaim the truth about God's way no matter whom you might offend in the process. So tell us your view. Is it right for us to give taxes to the Roman Emperor or not?"

Jesus, however, saw through their trick and replied, "Why are you trying to catch me up on this, you hypocrites? Bring me the coin required for the tax, so I can examine it."

They brought him a denarius, and he asked, "Whose head is this on it and whose inscription?"

"Caesar's," they answered.

"Very well then, pay Caesar what belongs to Caesar, and pay God what belongs to God."

His reply took them so completely by surprise that they had nothing more to say. Their attempt to trap him in public having failed, they went away and left him alone.

The Sadducees Propound a Question About the Resurrection

Next some Sadducees came up. (Their party teaches that there is no resurrection of the dead.) This was the question they put.

"Teacher, Moses laid it down in the Law that if a man's brother dies leaving a wife but no child the man must marry the widow and produce children for his brother. Now suppose there were seven brothers. The eldest took a wife and died childless. Then the second married her, and he too died without issue. The third did likewise and so on. Eventually all seven had died, none having had any children. Finally the woman died. Now in the resurrection whose wife will she be, considering that she was married to all seven?"

"Your solution to this puzzle is in error, because you are ignorant of both the scriptures and God's power. The men and women of this world marry and are given in marriage, but those judged worthy of the resurrection and a place in the world to come do not. They are like angels. They cannot die anymore. Having shared in the resurrection, they are children of God.

"And on whether there is a resurrection at all, Moses himself can be cited to prove there is. Haven't you read in the passage about the burning bush how God spoke to him and said, 'I am the God of Abraham, the God of Isaac, and the God of Jacob.' That means he is not God of the dead but of the living. So you are completely wrong."

"Well spoken, Teacher!" said some of the lawyers. And the crowds who heard all this were astonished at his teaching.

"Which Is the Great Commandment?"

When the Pharisees heard he had silenced the Sadducees they regrouped. One of them—a lawyer—having come upon the dispute and caught Jesus' thoughtful answer, put forward another test question.

"Teacher, which is the most important commandment in the Law?"

"The first and foremost is, 'Hear, O Israel! The
Lord our God is the only God. You must love the Lord
your God with all your heart, with all your soul, with all
your mind, and with all your strength.' The second is
like it. 'Love your neighbor as yourself.' On these two
commandments hangs everything in the Law and the
Prophets."

"Teacher," the lawyer said, "your point is well tak-
en. God is indeed one. There's no other God but him.
And to love him with all your heart, with all your understanding, and with all your strength, and to love your
neighbor as yourself, is far more than all the burnt
offerings and sacrifices anybody could possibly make."

When Jesus saw how perceptive his reply was, he
told him, "You are not far from the kingdom of God."

"Is the Messiah David's Son?"

While the Pharisees were assembled Jesus posed
them a question in turn.

"The lawyers say the Messiah is the Son of David.
What is your view? Whose son is he?"

"The Son of David," they replied.

"Then why did the Holy Spirit inspire David to call
him 'Lord'? David himself says in the book of Psalms,

'The Lord said to my Lord,
"Sit here at my right
Until I make your enemies
A footstool for your feet." '

If David himself thus calls the Messiah 'Lord,' how can
he be David's son?"

To this no one had a reply. And from that time on,
nobody dared put any more questions to Jesus.

The Lawyers and Pharisees Denounced

A great crowd had gathered and were listening eagerly. Within everybody's hearing Jesus taught his disciples, "The lawyers and the Pharisees sit in Moses' chair of authority, so pay heed to their instructions. But don't follow their example, because they don't practice what they preach. They make up heavy loads to tie on people's backs and then won't even lift a finger to help. They consume the property of widows and then compose long prayers to keep up appearances. They will face the sternest judgment!

"Everything they do is done for show. They like to stroll around in long robes with wide fringes and wear scripture verses on their foreheads and arms. They love the seats of honor at festivals and in the synagogues and to be bowed to in the marketplace and addressed as 'Rabbi.'

"But you are not to be called 'Rabbi.' You have one Rabbi, and you are all brothers. Likewise, don't call any man on earth 'Father.' You have one Father, and he's in heaven. And you are not to be called 'Teacher,' because you have only one teacher—the Messiah. The greatest among you will be your servant. Remember, whoever promotes himself will be humbled, and whoever humbles himself will be promoted."

Then he reproached the lawyers and Pharisees directly.

"Woe to you lawyers and Pharisees, you hypocrites! You have locked people out of the kingdom of heaven and thrown away the key of knowledge. You did not go in yourselves, and those who were on their way in, you stopped.

"Woe to you lawyers and Pharisees, you hypocrites! You travel over land and sea to make a single convert, and having won him over, you make him twice as much a child of hell as you yourselves.

"Woe to you, you blind guides! You tell people, 'If anybody swears by the Temple, that is not binding, but if he swears by the gold in the Temple he is bound by his oath.' Blind fools! Which is more important, the gold or the Temple that sanctifies it? You also say, 'If anybody swears by the altar, that is nothing, but if he swears by the offering that lies on the altar his oath is binding.' How can you be so blind? Which is more important, the offering or the altar that sanctifies it? To swear by the Temple is to swear both by it and by the one who dwells there. And to swear by heaven is to swear both by the throne of God and by its occupant.

"Woe to you lawyers and Pharisees, you hypocrites! You even pay tithes of the seasoning herbs, such as mint, rue, dill, and cumin, but overlook the weightier demands of the Law—justice, mercy, faith, and love of God. It is these you should have practiced, without neglecting the others. Blind guides! You strain off the tiniest gnat yet swallow a camel whole!

"Woe to you lawyers and Pharisees, you hypocrites! You scrub the outside of the cup and the dish, but inwardly you are full of robbery and greed. Blind Pharisee! Didn't the one who made the outside make the inside too? Clean out the inside by giving, and everything will be clean for you. Once the inside is clean, the outside will be clean too.

"Woe to you lawyers and Pharisees, you hypocrites! You are like unmarked graves over which people walk without knowing it. You are like whitewashed tombs. From the outside they look beautiful, but inside they are full of the bones of the dead and all kinds of rotten filth. So it is with you. On the outside you look like honest and upright men, but inside you are brimming with hypocrisy and evil.

"Woe to you lawyers and Pharisees, you hypocrites! You build up the tombs of the prophets and decorate the monuments of the saints, declaring, 'If we had been alive in our forefathers' time we would never have taken part with them in murdering the prophets.' Thus you acknowledge yourselves to be the murderers' offspring. They committed the murders and you provide the tombs! Go on then and finish what your ancestors started!

"You snakes, you offspring of vipers, how can you escape being condemned to hell? This is why the Wisdom of God said, 'I will send them prophets and messengers, some of whom they will persecute and kill.' Thus on you will fall the guilt of all the shedding of innocent blood on earth, from the blood of innocent Abel to that of Zechariah, whom you murdered between the sanctuary and the altar. Indeed, I tell you this generation will have to answer for it all!"

As Jesus was leaving, the lawyers and Pharisees launched a vigorous counterattack, to provoke him to further speech on lots of things. They were just lying in wait for him, to catch him in a trap of his own words.

The Poor Widow's Gift

Jesus sat down opposite the Temple treasury and watched the crowd put in their gifts. Many of the rich gave large sums. Then a poor widow came by and dropped in two little copper coins, together barely worth a penny. Jesus called his disciples' attention.

"Believe me, this poor widow has put in more than all of them. They, with more than enough, gave out of wealth. But she, with nothing to spare, gave everything she had—her whole living.''

Jesus' Final Public Appeal

Some Greeks were among those who had come up to worship at the festival. They sought out Philip (who was from Bethsaida in Galilee) and told him, "Sir, we should like to see Jesus." Philip informed Andrew, and the two reported the request to Jesus. This was the answer Jesus gave them.

"The time has come for the Son of Man to be glorified. I tell you, unless a grain of wheat falls into the ground and dies, it remains a single, solitary grain. But if it dies, it multiplies. Whoever loves his life loses it, but whoever in this world hates his life will keep it for eternity. If anyone would serve me he must follow me. Where I am, my servant will be too. And anyone who serves me the Father will honor.

"Now my soul is in turmoil! What shall I say?—'Father, save me from this hour'? No! It is for this very reason I have come to this hour. Father, bring glory to your name!"

A voice sounded from heaven. "I have done so and will do so again!"

The crowd standing there heard it and said it was thunder. Others said, "An angel reassured him!"

"This voice spoke for your sake, not mine," Jesus told them. "The judgment of this world is *now*. It is now that the Prince of this world will be overthrown! And I when I am lifted up from the earth will draw all people to myself." (By this he indicated the kind of death he was going to die.)

The crowd answered back, "We have been taught that the Law says the Messiah stays forever. So how can you say the Son of Man must be lifted up? Who is this Son of Man you're talking about?"

"The light is still with you but not for long. Go your way while you have the light, so the darkness will not overtake you. One who journeys in the dark doesn't know where he's going. Believe in the light, then, while you've got it, so you will become children of light."

After this Jesus left the crowds and kept out of their sight. In spite of all the many signs he had performed in their presence they still did not believe in him. The words of the prophet Isaiah were destined to come true:

> "Lord, who has believed what we reported,
> And to whom has the Lord's power been
>   revealed?"

Thus it was that they were unable to believe, just as Isaiah also predicted:

> "He has blinded their eyes
> And closed their minds,
> To keep them from seeing with their eyes
> And perceiving with their minds,
> And turning to me for healing."

Isaiah said this because he saw Jesus' glory and spoke about him.

Nevertheless quite a few even among those in authority believed in Jesus but would not acknowledge him for fear that the Pharisees would have them banned from the synagogue. They cared more for their reputation among people than for the honor that comes from God.

This prompted Jesus to cry out, "Whoever believes in me is believing, not in me but in the one who sent me. And whoever sees me is seeing the one who sent me.

"I have come into the world as light, so that whoever believes in me won't stay in darkness. But if anybody hears my words and fails to keep them I won't be his judge. I came, not to judge the world but to save it. The one who rejects me and my message already has a judge. The word I have spoken will be his judge on the last day. I have never spoken on my own authority. The Father who sent me commanded me himself what to say and how to speak. And I know his command brings eternal life. What I say, then, I speak as the Father has directed me."

IX

Jesus Prepares His Disciples for His Death

Signs of Things to Come

As Jesus was leaving the Temple one of his disciples remarked, "Look, Teacher, what fine stones and offerings! What wonderful buildings!"

"You see these great buildings?" said Jesus. "I tell you the time is coming when not one stone here will be left on top of another. Everything will be demolished."

Later while Jesus was seated on the Mount of Olives facing the Temple he was questioned privately by Peter, James, John, and Andrew.

"Tell us, Teacher, when is all this to take place? And what will give us warning that it's time for your coming and the end of the age?"

"Watch out," Jesus began, "and don't let anybody

mislead you. A great many will come in my name, saying, 'I am the Messiah!' and 'The time has come!' And they will mislead lots of people. Don't go running after them. And when you hear of wars and rumors of wars, don't be alarmed. This must happen first, but it is not yet the end."

Then he told them, "Nation will rise against nation and kingdom against kingdom. There will be great earthquakes in various places, and famines and plagues. Terrible portents will fill the skies. But all this is only the beginning of the birthpangs.

"Keep yourselves on guard. Before all this happens they will seize you and persecute you. They will hand you over to councils and prisons and whip you in their synagogues. You will be dragged before governors and kings, accused on my account. This will be your opportunity to testify before them and the Gentiles.

"When they bring you before the synagogues and rulers and authorities, don't worry about how to speak or what to say. Make up your minds not to compose your defense in advance. I shall give you a power of speech and a wisdom that none of your opponents will be able to resist or rebut. Speak whatever God gives you at the time. It won't be you speaking but the Holy Spirit speaking through you.

"You will be handed over by friends and relatives. Even brothers will betray each other to death, and the father his child. Children will turn against their parents and have them put to death. And you will be hated by everyone for owning my name. Many will fall away and betray each other and hate each other. False prophets will abound, leading great numbers astray. Evil will spread so wide that most people's love will grow cold.

But not a hair of your head will perish. By standing firm to the end you will win through to life.

"When you are persecuted in one town, escape to the next. I tell you, you will not get through all the towns of Israel before the Son of Man comes. And this good news of the kingdom must first be proclaimed throughout the whole world, as a testimony to all nations, and then the end will come.

"But when you see Jerusalem surrounded by armies you can be sure her destruction is near. And when you see the 'abomination of desolation,' of which the prophet Daniel spoke, standing in the holy place, those in Judea must take to the hills. Those inside the city must leave it, and those out in the country must not come in. On that day a person up on the roof with his belongings in the house must not come back down inside to get anything, and anybody in the field must not turn back for his cloak. Remember Lot's wife!

"This is the time of retribution when the scriptures will all be fulfilled. How sad for pregnant women in those days! And for nursing mothers! Pray it won't happen in winter, because those days will bring such great distress as has never been before, since the beginning of creation, and will never be again. If the Lord had not cut short that time, nobody would survive. But for the sake of his chosen ones he cut it short. A terrible judgment will fall on this people. They will be put to the sword and carried captive into all countries. The Gentiles will trample Jerusalem underfoot until their age has run its course.

"The time will come when you'll long to see one of the days of the Son of Man, but you won't see it. Then if anybody says to you, 'Look! Here's the Messiah!' or

'Look! There he is!', don't believe it. Don't go. Don't follow them. Imposters will come claiming to be messiahs or prophets, and they'll produce signs and wonders to deceive even God's chosen ones if possible. But you be on guard. I have warned you of it all in advance. So if they tell you, 'He is there in the desert,' don't go dashing out. And if they say, 'He is here in the inner room,' don't believe it, because the coming of the Son of Man will be like the flash of lightning that lights up the sky from one horizon to the other."

"But when, Lord?" they asked him.

"Remember," he replied, "to find a corpse you have to watch and see where the vultures gather.

"In those days, after that distress, the sun will turn dark, the moon will stop shining, and stars will fall from the sky. On earth whole nations will despair, not knowing which way to turn from the roaring sea and the raging tides. And people will faint with fear and foreboding at what's happening to the world, because the powers of the heavens will be shaken.

"Then in the sky will appear the sign that heralds the Son of Man. All the tribes of the earth will cry out. They will see the Son of Man coming on the clouds of heaven with great power and glory. With a trumpet blast he will send out the angels to the four winds and gather together his chosen ones, from the farthest bounds of earth to the farthest reaches of heaven.

"Now when these things begin to happen, look up and hold your heads high, because your redemption is near. Learn a lesson from the fig tree. When its tender green shoots come out and sprout into leaf you can see for yourselves summer is nigh. Likewise when you see all these things happening you know he is close by, even at the gates. I tell you this generation won't pass away before all these things take place. Heaven and earth will pass away, but my words will not. The exact day and hour, however, nobody knows, not even the angels in heaven, not even the Son, but only the Father.

"Just as it was in the time of Noah, so it will be in the time of the Son of Man. Everybody kept on eating and drinking and marrying right up to the day when Noah entered the ark. They were totally oblivious until the flood came and swept them all away. So it will be when the Son of Man comes.

"And just as it was in Lot's time too. Everybody kept on eating and drinking, buying and selling, planting and building. But on the day Lot left Sodom fire and sulphur rained down from heaven and destroyed them all.

"That's how it will be on the day the Son of Man is revealed. I tell you, that night there will be two asleep in the same bed. One will be taken; the other, left behind. Two men will be in the field. One is taken and one is left. Two women will be at the mill grinding meal together. One will be taken and the other left."

"So Be Prepared!"

"Always stand ready with belts buckled and lamps lit. Be on watch, be alert, because you don't know what time to expect it. Don't let your minds be dulled by dissipation and drunkenness and the cares of this life so that the Great Day closes on you suddenly like a trap! On all the earth's inhabitants, the wide world over, it will come.

"Think of it this way. It is like when a man is away at a wedding feast. He has left his servants in charge of the house, each with his own work to do, and has given the doorman orders to keep a lookout for him, ready to let him in the very moment he arrives and knocks. How happy those servants the master finds awake when he comes! I tell you he will hitch up his belt, seat them at the table, and come wait on them.

"So be on the alert, praying always for strength to pass safely through these coming troubles and to stand upright before the Son of Man. Remember, you don't know when the master of the house is coming, whether in the evening or at midnight, just before dawn or in the morning. Don't let him come on you suddenly and catch you asleep!"

The Parables of the Burglar and the Servant in Charge

"Think about this. If the homeowner had known what time of night to expect the burglar he would have been wide awake and kept the thief from breaking into his house. So hold yourselves ready, because the Son of Man is coming at a time you don't expect."

"Lord," said Peter, "are you telling this parable specially for us, or do you mean it for everybody?"

"What I say to you, I say to everyone. Stay awake!

"But how about the servant charged with supervision of his master's household staff, to see to it they are fed at the proper time? Will he prove faithful and wise? How happy he will be if found at his job when his master comes! I tell you he will be put in charge of all his master's property. But if he turns out to be a bad servant and says to himself, 'My master is delayed,' and begins to bully the other servants and the maids, and to eat, drink, and carouse with his drunken friends, then his master will arrive on an unexpected day at an unknown hour and cut him in two. Thus he will find his place with the disobedient and the hypocrites—the place of wailing and gritting of teeth.

"And the servant who knew his master's wishes yet made no attempt to carry them out will get a severe whipping. But the one who didn't know and who did what otherwise deserved a beating will receive a lighter punishment. Of everyone to whom much is given, much will be required. And the more one has had entrusted to him, the more will be demanded of him."

The Parable of the Ten Bridesmaids

"The coming of the kingdom of heaven may be compared to the case of ten bridesmaids who took their lamps and went to meet the bridegroom. Five of them were foolish and five prudent. The foolish ones carried no oil with their lamps, while the wise each brought along a flask full with theirs. Since the bridegroom was delayed, they all dozed off to sleep.

"At midnight a shout rang out, 'The bridegroom is here! Come out to meet him!' The girls all jumped up and trimmed their lamps. The foolish ones said to the wise, 'Give us some of your oil. Our lamps are going out.' 'No,' the wise ones replied, 'maybe there won't be enough for us both. You had better go to the shop and buy some of your own.' So off went the foolish girls to make their purchase.

"While they were gone the bridegroom came, and those who were ready went in with him to the wedding feast. And the door was locked. Later the other five arrived. 'Sir, Sir!' they called out, 'Let us in!' 'But I really don't know you,' the bridegroom replied.

"So keep alert, because you don't know either the day or the hour."

The Last Judgment

"When the Son of Man comes in his glory and all the angels with him he will sit in state on his throne, and all the nations will be gathered before him. He'll divide them into two groups just as a shepherd separates the sheep from the goats. The sheep he will put at his right hand but the goats at his left.

"Then the King will say to those at his right, 'Come, you who have my Father's blessing! Come possess the kingdom prepared for you since the creation of the world. I was hungry and you gave me food. I was thirsty and you gave me a drink. I was a stranger and you took me in. I was naked and you clothed me. I was sick and you came to my help. I was in prison and you visited me.'

"Then the righteous will reply, 'Lord, when did we ever see you hungry and feed you, or thirsty and give you a drink? When did we ever see you a stranger and take you in, or naked and clothe you? When did we ever see you sick or in prison and visit you?' The King will answer back, 'I'm telling you the truth. Whenever you did it for one of these my brothers, no matter how humble, you did it for me!'

"Then he'll say to those on his left, 'Out of my sight, you accursed! Away to the eternal fire ready for the devil and his angels! When I was hungry you gave me nothing to eat; when thirsty, nothing to drink. I was a stranger and you barred your door against me; naked and you wouldn't clothe me; sick and in prison and you never visited me.'

"Then they too will reply, 'Lord, when did we ever see you hungry or thirsty or a stranger or naked or sick or in prison and fail to come to your aid?' And his answer will be, 'I tell you indeed, whenever you failed to do it for any of these, even the least, you failed to do it for me.'

"These, then, will be sent off to eternal punishment; but the righteous, to eternal life."

Jesus Predicts His Crucifixion

When Jesus had finished all these teachings he told his disciples, "You realize that in two days' time the Passover is coming and the Festival of Unleavened Bread, and the Son of Man is being handed over for crucifixion."

The chief priests, the lawyers, and the elders of the nation met in the palace of the high priest—Caiaphas—and conferred together on a scheme to get Jesus arrested secretly and put to death.

"It had better not be during the festival," they said, "or there may be rioting among the people."

Thirty Silver Coins

Then Satan entered Judas called Iscariot, who was one of the twelve. He went to the chief priests and the officers of the Temple guard and talked with them about delivering Jesus into their power.

"What will you give me to hand him over to you?" he asked them.

They were delighted with his offer and agreed to pay him thirty silver coins. From that time on he looked for a good opportunity to carry out his bargain without the crowds being present.

The Preparations for the Passover

At last the day was coming on which the lambs for the Passover meal were sacrificed. The Festival of Unleavened Bread was about to begin.

Jesus told Peter and John to go prepare the Passover meal for them so they could eat it.

"Where would you have us prepare it?" they inquired.

"Look, as you go into the city a man will meet you carrying a waterpot. Follow him into the house he enters and tell the head of the household, 'The Teacher says, "My time is at hand. My disciples and I will celebrate the Passover at your house. Where is the room reserved for us?" ' He will show you a large upstairs room all furnished and ready. Make the necessary preparations there."

The disciples set out for the city and found everything just as Jesus had said. And they prepared the Passover meal.

Jesus Arrives with the Twelve

With the coming of evening Jesus arrived with the twelve and took his place at the table with them.

"I wanted very much to eat this Passover with you before I suffer, because, I tell you, I will not celebrate it until it finds its fulfillment in the kingdom of God.

"You are the ones who have stood firmly by me in my times of trial. And just as my Father appointed me a kingdom, I make the same covenant with you. You will eat and drink at my table in my kingdom and sit on thrones to govern the twelve tribes of Israel."

A jealous dispute erupted over which of them took precedence. Jesus broke in.

"The kings of the Gentiles lord it over their subjects, and those in authority get themselves titled their country's benefactors. But not so with you. Rather, the greatest among you must bear himself like the youngest; and the leader, like a servant."

Jesus Washes His Disciples' Feet

It was before the Passover festival. Jesus knew his time had come to leave this world and go to the Father.

Having always loved his own who were in the world, he now loved them to the uttermost.

The devil had already put it into the mind of Judas son of Simon Iscariot to betray Jesus. So during supper Jesus, knowing that the Father had entrusted everything to him and that he had come from God and was going back to God, got up from the table and, laying down his clothes, wrapped a towel around his waist. He filled a washbasin with water and began to bathe the disciples' feet and dry them with the towel. He came to Simon Peter.

"*You*, Lord, washing *my* feet?"

"You don't understand now what I'm doing, but one day you will."

"You will never, at any time, wash my feet!"

"If I don't, then you take no part in me."

"In that case, Lord, don't just wash my feet. Go on and wash my hands and head too."

"One who is bathed needs no further washing. He is completely clean. And you are clean, all but one." (Jesus added these last words because he knew who was going to betray him.)

When he had finished washing their feet, taken his clothes, and resumed his place he asked, "Tell me who is greater, the one who sits down to eat or the servant who waits on him? Why, the one who sits down, of course. Do you know what I have done to you? You call me 'Teacher' and 'Lord' and rightly so, because that is what I am. Yet here I am among you as a servant. I your Lord and Teacher have just washed your feet. You then ought to do likewise for each other. I have set you an example. You are to do as I have done to you. Believe me, a servant is not above his master nor a messenger above the one who sent him. Now that you know these things you will do well to put them into practice.

"I am not talking about all of you. I know whom I have chosen. But the scripture must come true that says, 'The one who ate bread with me has turned against me.' I tell you this now before it happens, so that when it does happen you will believe that I am."

Jesus Points Out His Betrayer

Having thus spoken, Jesus was deeply disturbed.

"It's the truth, I tell you!" he exclaimed. "One of you is going to betray me! Yes, one whose hand is right here on the table with mine."

The disciples were dismayed at this and looked at each other bewildered. To whom was he referring?

One by one they began asking, "Surely not me, Lord?"

"It is one of the twelve, who has dipped his hand in the same dish with me. True, the Son of Man is bound to walk the path laid out for him in the scriptures, but woe to the man by whom he is betrayed! It would be better for that man if he had never been born."

One of the group—the disciple Jesus loved—was lying close beside Jesus. Simon Peter caught his attention and whispered to him, "Tell us who it is he means."

From that position close by Jesus' side the disciple asked him, "Who is it, Lord?"

"It is the one to whom I give this piece of bread after I have dipped it in the dish," Jesus told him.

Dipping the bread in the dish, he handed it to Judas the son of Simon Iscariot.

"What?" said Judas. "I, Rabbi?"

"The words are yours," Jesus replied.

As soon as Judas took it Satan entered him, and Jesus told him, "Do quickly what you are going to do."

(Nobody at the table knew why he had said this to Judas. Some thought that because Judas was the treasurer Jesus was sending him off to buy what they needed for the festival or to make some gift to the poor.)

Judas, having taken the bread, got right up and went out. It was night.

The Memorial of the Last Supper

As they were eating, Jesus took bread and after giving thanks to God broke it and gave it to them.

"Take and eat it. This is my body which is for you. Do this in memory of me."

In the same way too he took the cup after supper and, having offered thanks to God, handed it around with these words.

"All of you, drink from it. This cup is God's new covenant sealed with my blood, shed for many for the forgiveness of sins. Whenever you drink it, do this in memory of me. I tell you, from now on I will not drink the fruit of the vine till the kingdom of God comes."

"Before the Cock Crows, You Will Disown Me"

"The Son of Man will now be glorified, and in him God will be glorified. And if God is glorified in him God will also glorify the Son of Man in himself, and he will do it quickly.

"My children, I won't be with you much longer. You will look for me, but what I told the Jews I now tell you, 'Where I am going you cannot come.'

"I give you a new commandment. Love each other just as I have loved you. This is how everybody will know you are my disciples—if you have this love for each other."

"Where are you going, Lord?" Simon Peter asked him.

"Where I am going you cannot follow me now, but one day you will."

"Why can't I follow you now, Lord?"

"Simon, Simon! Listen, Satan has demanded permission to sift all of you like wheat. But I have prayed for you, Simon, that your faith won't fail. And when you have come to yourself you must lend strength to your brethren."

He told them, "Tonight all of you will fall away because of me. It stands written, 'I will strike the shepherd down and the sheep of his flock will be scattered.' But after I am raised to life I will go on to Galilee ahead of you."

"I will never fall away," Peter objected, "even though all the rest do. Lord, I'm ready to go to prison with you! I'm ready to die for you!"

"Are you really ready to die for me? I'm telling you the truth, Peter. This very night before the rooster crows twice you will deny three times that you even know me."

"I will never disown you," Peter insisted vehemently, "even if I have to die with you!" And all the disciples said the same thing.

"That time I sent you out barefoot without purse or pack, were you ever short of anything?"

"Not a thing," they replied.

"Well, things are different now. Whoever has a purse had better take it with him, and his pack too, and if he has no sword he had better sell his coat and buy one. I tell you scripture says, 'He was counted among the lawbreakers,' and these words must find fulfillment in me. Indeed, everything written about me is coming true."

"Look, Lord," they said, "we have two swords here."

"Enough of this!" he exclaimed.

Jesus' Farewell to His Disciples

"Put your hearts at ease. Trust in God. Trust in me too. There are many places to live in my Father's house. If it were not so, I would have told you. I am going in order to prepare a place for you. And after I go and prepare a place for you I shall return and take you to me, so that where I am you can be too. And you know the way to get where I am going."

"Lord," said Thomas, "we don't know where you're going, so how can we know the way?"

"I am the way, I am the truth, I am the life. Nobody comes to the Father except by me. If you know me you will know my Father too. From now on you do know him and have seen him."

"Lord," said Philip, "show us the Father and we will be satisfied."

"Have I been with you all this time, Philip, and you still don't know me? Whoever has seen me has seen the Father. So how can you say, 'Show us the Father'? Don't you believe, Philip, that I am in the Father and the Father is in me? I am not myself the source of the words I speak to you. It is the Father who lives in me doing his works. Believe me when I say I am in the Father and the Father is in me, or else accept the evidence of the works themselves.

"I'm telling you the truth. Whoever believes in me will do the same works, yes, and even greater ones because I am going to the Father. Indeed, I will do whatever you ask in my name, so that the Father may be glorified in the Son. If you ask anything in my name I will do it.

"If you love me you will obey my commands. I will ask the Father, and he will give you someone else to be your Counsellor and Helper who will be with you forever—the Spirit of truth. The world can't receive him because it neither sees him nor knows him. But you know him, because he lives with you and will be in you.

"I will not leave you orphaned. I will come back to you. In a little while the world won't see me anymore, but you will see me. Because I live you will live too. Then you will know that I am in my Father and you are in me and I am in you. Whoever has my commands and obeys them, he is the one who loves me. And whoever loves me will be loved by my Father, and I will love him and disclose myself to him."

Judas (the other one, not Iscariot) asked him, "Lord, how come you will disclose yourself only to us and not to the world?"

"If anyone loves me he will keep my word, and my Father will love him and we will come to him and live with him. Anyone who does not love me does not keep my words. And what you are hearing is not mine. It is from the Father who sent me.

"These things I have told you while I am still with you. But the Helper—the Holy Spirit the Father will send in my name—will teach you everything and will call to mind all the things I have told you.

"Peace is my parting gift to you—my own peace, such as the world cannot give. Put your hearts at ease. Banish fear. You heard me say, 'I am going away and I shall come back to you.' If you loved me you would be glad I am going to the Father, because the Father is greater than I am. I have told you this now before it happens, so that when it does happen you will believe. I will not talk with you much longer because the Prince of this world is coming. He has no power over me, but the world must be shown I love the Father and do exactly as he commands.

"Get up. Let us leave this place.

"I am the real vine, and my Father is the gardener. Every barren branch in me he cuts off, and every one that does bear fruit he prunes so it will bear more. You are already purged by the word I have spoken to you. Live in me just as I live in you. No branch can bear fruit by itself. It must stay joined to the vine. You cannot bear fruit either unless you live in me.

"I am the vine. You are the branches. Whoever lives in me as I live in him will bear fruit in abundance. Apart from me you can do nothing. Whoever does not live in me is thrown out like a cut branch and dries up. And dead branches are gathered, thrown on the fire, and burned. If you live in me and my words live in you, ask whatever you will, and it will be done for you. This is my Father's glory that you bear fruit in abundance and thus prove to be my disciples.

"Just as the Father has loved me, I have loved you. Live in my love. If you obey my commands you will live in my love, just as I have obeyed my Father's commands and live in his love. I have told you these things so that my joy may be in you and your joy complete.

"This is my commandment. Love each other just as I have loved you. It is the ultimate love—laying down one's life for one's friends.

"You are my friends if you do what I command. I don't call you servants anymore, because a servant doesn't know what his master's doing. Instead I have called you friends, because I have disclosed everything to you I heard from my Father. But you didn't choose me. I chose you. And I appointed you to go and bear fruit, lasting fruit, so that whatever you ask in my name the Father may give you. This, then, is what I command you. Love each other.

"If the world hates you, remember it hated me first. If you belonged to the world the world would love you like its own. But because you do not belong to the world, because I chose you out of it, that is why the world hates you. Remember what I told you—'A servant is not above his master.' If they persecuted me they will persecute you; if they kept my word they will keep yours too. But it's on my account that they will do all this to you, because they do not know the one who sent me.

"If I had not come and spoken to them they would not be guilty of sin, but now they have no excuse for their sin. Whoever hates me hates my Father too. If I had not done the works among them nobody else ever did, they would not be guilty of sin. As it is, they have seen what I did and they have hated both me and my Father. This had to be, however, so that this text in their Law should come true: 'They hated me without reason.'

"But when the Helper comes—the Spirit of truth who comes from the Father—he will bear witness to me. I will send him to you from the Father. And you are witnesses too, because you have been with me from the very beginning.

"I have told you all this to keep you from falling away. They will kick you out of the synagogue. Indeed the time is coming when anybody who kills you will think he's serving God. And they will do this because they have not known either the Father or me. But I have told you these things so that when their time comes you will remember my warning. I didn't tell you at first because I was with you. But now I'm going to the one who sent me.

"None of you asks where I'm going, yet you're drowned in grief because of what I've told you. I'm telling you the truth, though. It's better for you I go, because if I don't, the Helper won't come to you. But if I go I will send him to you. And when he comes he will convince the world of right and wrong and judgment. He will convict them of wrong by their failure to believe in me. He will convince them that right's on my side by showing that I go to the Father when I pass from your sight. And he will convince them of God's judgment by showing that the Prince of this world stands condemned.

"I have a lot more to tell you, but the burden now would be too great for you to bear. When the Spirit of truth comes he will guide you into all the truth, because he won't speak on his own authority but will tell only what he hears, and he will make plain to you the things to come. He will glorify me, because he will take what is mine and make it plain to you. Everything the Father has is mine, and that is why I said the Spirit will take what is mine and make it plain to you.

"In just a little while you won't see me anymore. Then a little while later you will see me."

Some of his disciples said to each other, "What does he mean by this? He tells us, 'In a little while you won't see me, and then a little later you will see me.' And he says, 'It is because I'm going to the Father.' What is this 'little while' he mentions? We don't know what he's talking about!"

Jesus knew they were wanting to question him, so he spoke again.

"Are you asking yourselves what I meant about it being a little while and you wouldn't see me, and then a little later and you would see me? I'm telling you the truth. You will be weeping and wailing, but the world will be glad. You will be drowned in grief, but your grief will turn to joy. A woman in labor experiences pain because her time has come. But after her delivery she forgets the anguish in her joy that a baby's born into the world. So it is with you. Now you're sad at heart, but I shall see you again, and then you will be full of joy—the kind nobody can rob you of. When that day comes you won't ask me any questions.

"I'm telling you the truth. The Father will give you anything you ask in my name. So far you have asked nothing in my name. Ask and you will receive, so your joy will be complete.

"I've been talking to you in figures of speech. The time is coming when I won't use them anymore but will tell you about the Father in plain words. When that day comes you will ask in my name, and I don't say I will intercede for you. You have loved me and believed I came from the Father. So he loves you himself.

"I did come from the Father and I have come into the world. Now I am leaving the world and going to the Father."

"Why, you are speaking plainly now," said the disciples. "This is no figure of speech. We're now sure you know everything. You don't need to be questioned. Because of this we believe you came from God."

"Do you really believe now? Look, the time is coming, in fact it is already here, when you will be scattered each to his own home and I shall be left alone. Yet I am not really alone because the Father is with me. I have told you these things so that in me you will have peace. In the world you have trouble in store. But take heart! The victory is mine. I have defeated the world!"

Jesus Prays for His Disciples

When Jesus had spoken these words he looked up to heaven.

"Father, the time has come. Glorify your Son so that the Son may glorify you. You have made him sovereign over all creation, to give eternal life to the whole group you have given him. And this is eternal life—for them to know you, the only true God, and the one you have sent, Jesus the Messiah. I glorified you on earth. I have completed the work you gave me to do. O Father! Now glorify me in your own presence with that same glory I had with you before the world was formed.

"I have made you known to the men you gave me out of the world. They belonged to you, and you gave them to me. They have kept your word, and now they know that all your gifts have come to me from you. I have given them the words you gave me, and they have received them. They know for sure I came from you. They have believed you sent me.

"I pray for them. I don't pray for the world but for those you have given me, because they belong to you. All mine are yours, and yours are mine. And through them I am glorified. Now I am coming to you. I am not in the world anymore, but they are in the world. O Holy Father, keep them in you, those you have given me, so they may be one just as you and I are one. While I was with them I kept them in you, those you have given me. I have protected them, and not one is lost but the man who had to be lost in order that scripture might come true. Now I am on my way to you, but while I am still in the world I speak these words, so that they will have my joy fulfilled in their hearts.

"I have given them your message, and the world

hated them because they are strangers in the world just as I am. I don't ask you to take them out of the world but to keep them safe from the evil one. Just as I don't belong to the world, they don't belong to it. Consecrate them in the truth. Your word is truth. Just as you sent me into the world, I have sent them into the world. And for their sake I consecrate myself in order that they too may be consecrated in truth.

"It is not for these alone I pray but also for those who will come to believe through their testimony. May they all be one. O Father! May they be in us just as you are in me and I am in you, so that the world may believe you sent me. The glory you have given me I have given them, so that they may be one just as you and I are one. I in them and you in me, let them become perfectly one in order that the world may know that you did send me and have loved it just as you've loved me.

"O Father! These you have given me, I want them to be with me where I am, to see my glory—the glory you have given me because you loved me before the creation of the world. O righteous Father! The world has not known you, but I have known you, and these know you sent me. I made you known to them and will continue to do so, in order that the love you have had for me may be in them and I in them."

In the Garden of Gethsemane

When Jesus had spoken these words and they had sung a hymn he went outside and headed as usual for the Mount of Olives. The disciples accompanied him and they crossed the Kidron ravine. There was a garden there called Gethsemane, and he and the disciples went in. The place was known to Judas his betrayer, because Jesus often met there with his disciples.

Once inside, Jesus told them to pray to avoid temptation. Then taking with him Peter, and James and John the sons of Zebedee, he instructed the others, "Sit down here while I go over there and pray."

With these three he went off about a stone's throw and knelt down. Overwhelmed with anguish and distress he turned to them.

"My heart is about to break with sorrow. Stay here and keep watch with me."

He went on a little further and fell with his face to the ground and prayed that if it were possible this hour might pass him by.

"*Abba*! ('Father') To you all things are possible. If you are willing, take this cup away from me. Yet not my will but yours be done."

An angel from heaven appeared to him and strengthened him. In agony he prayed even more urgently, and his sweat was like big drops of blood falling to the ground.

When he got up from prayer and came over he found the disciples asleep, worn out with grief.

"What, Simon, asleep?" he said to Peter. "Could you not keep watch with me just an hour? Stay awake and pray to avoid temptation. The spirit is willing, but the flesh is weak."

Again a second time Jesus went off and prayed, "My Father, if it is not possible for this cup to be taken away without my drinking it, your will be done."

Again he came back to the disciples and found them asleep. Unable to keep their eyes open, they did not know what to say to him.

He left them and went away again and prayed the third time, saying the same words as before. Then he returned to the disciples and spoke.

"Still sleeping and resting? Well, no matter. The time has come. Look! The Son of Man is betrayed into the power of sinners. Get up. Let us go. See, the traitor is upon us!"

The Arrest, Trial, Crucifixion, and Burial

The Kiss of Judas

While Jesus was still speaking, Judas—one of the twelve—arrived at the garden accompanied by a great mob of soldiers and Temple guards provided by the chief priests and elders of the people, the lawyers, and the Pharisees. They came equipped with lanterns and torches and armed with swords and clubs. Jesus, knowing everything that was going to happen to him, went out to meet them.

The traitor had agreed with them on a signal. "The one I kiss is your man. Seize him and carry him off under guard."

When, therefore, he reached the spot he hailed

Jesus. "Peace be with you, Rabbi!" And he stepped forward to kiss him.

"Judas," said Jesus, "would you betray the Son of Man with a kiss?"

And Judas kissed him.

As the crowd came up, Jesus spoke out.

"Who is it you want?"

"Jesus of Nazareth!" they said.

"I am!" came the reply, and at that they fell back, losing their footing.

"Who is it you want?" Jesus asked again.

"Jesus of Nazareth."

"I told you I am he. So if I am the man you want, let these others go." (He said this to make good his word, "I did not lose a single one of those you gave me.")

When his followers saw what was coming they cried, "Lord, shall we use our swords?"

Simon Peter reached for his, drew it, and struck the high priest's slave (whose name was Malchus), cutting off his right ear. But Jesus stopped them short.

"No more of this! Peter, sheathe your sword! All those who take the sword will die by the sword. Don't you know I could appeal to my Father who would immediately send more than twelve legions of angels to my aid? But how then could the scriptures be fulfilled that say this must happen? This is the cup the Father has given me. You think I won't drink it?"

He touched the wounded man's ear and healed him. Then he addressed the chief priests and elders and captains of the Temple guard who had come to seize him.

"Do you take me for a bandit that you have to come out with swords and clubs to capture me? Day after day

I sat with you in the Temple teaching, and you never laid hands on me. But all this has happened to fulfill what the prophets wrote. The hour belongs to you and the power of darkness."

Turning to Judas, he said, "Friend, do what you are here for."

They came up and grabbed him and held him fast. Then the disciples all deserted him and ran away.

A certain young man with nothing but a linen cloth wrapped around him followed Jesus. They grabbed him too, but he slipped out of the cloth and ran away naked.

An Informal Interrogation

After the company with their commander and the Jewish police had bound Jesus they brought him first to Annas, because he was the father-in-law of Caiaphas who was high priest that year. (It was Caiaphas who had counseled the Jews that it would be better if one man died for the whole people.)

The high priest then questioned Jesus about his disciples and his teaching. This was Jesus' reply.

'I have spoken openly to the world. My teaching always took place in the synagogues and the Temple, where all Jews congregate. I have said nothing in secret. So why compel me to be a witness in my own trial? Interrogate the people who've heard me. Ask them what I told them. They know what I said."

At these words one of the guards standing by slapped him. "How dare you talk like that to the high priest!"

"If I have spoken incorrectly, present evidence of it. But if I am correct in what I said, why hit me?"

Annas then sent him still tied up to Caiaphas the high priest.

The Examination Before the Sanhedrin

Jesus was led off to the high priest's house where the chief priests, elders, and lawyers were assembling.

The men guarding Jesus made fun of him. Some of them began to spit in his face and beat him with their fists. They blindfolded him and slapped him around, crying, "Now, Messiah! If you're a prophet, tell us who hit you?" And they went on like, that heaping insults on him.

When finally the assembly was convened the chief priests and the whole Council tried to find some allegation against Jesus on which to frame the charge of a capital offense but were unable to find any. Many witnesses came forward with false evidence, but their stories did not agree.

At last two stood up and told this lie about him. "We heard him say, 'I shall tear down this Temple made by men, and in three days I shall build another one not made by human hands.'" Not even they, however, could make their stories agree.

At this point the high priest stood up in his place and questioned Jesus.

"Have you no answer to the accusations these witnesses bring against you?"

Jesus, however, was silent and made no defense.

Finally the high priest demanded, "On your oath by the living God I charge you to tell us. Are you the Messiah, the Son of the Blessed One?"

"If I tell you what I am, you won't believe, and if I ask you what you mean, you won't answer. But in the future you will see the Son of Man seated at the right hand of the Almighty and coming on the clouds of heaven."

"You are the Son of God, then?" they all said.

"The words are yours," was his response.

At this the high priest tore his robes.

"Blasphemy!" he exclaimed. "What more testimony do we need? You have just heard his blasphemy from his own lips. What is your decision?"

"He is guilty," they answered, "and should die!"

Peter's Denial

Meanwhile Simon Peter had followed at a distance along with another disciple. Now this other disciple happened to be an acquaintance of the high priest, so when Jesus went in he too was allowed inside the courtyard of the high priest's house. But Peter stayed outside at the gate. This disciple the high priest knew went back out, spoke to the girl at the gate, and brought Peter in.

It was cold, so the slaves and guards had built a charcoal fire in the middle of the courtyard and were huddled around it warming themselves. So Peter went over and joined them, warming himself, intending to see the end of it all.

While he was sitting there down in the courtyard the girl who kept the gate came over and peered at his face in the firelight.

"You too," she said, "were with the Galilean, Jesus of Nazareth. Aren't you one of his disciples too?"

He denied it in front of all of them, muttering, "Woman, I don't know him . . . I don't understand what you mean." And he walked out into the passageway.

The servant girl saw him there and began to repeat to the bystanders, "This man was with Jesus of Nazareth. He is one of them."

As Peter came and stood by the fire to warm himself they asked him, "Aren't you too one of his disciples?"

Again he denied it, this time with an oath. "I am not, sir! I don't know the man."

After about an hour one of the high priest's slaves —a relative of the one whose ear Peter had cut off— stopped by and insisted, "Didn't I see you with him in the garden?"

Another bystander spoke up. "Why of course this man was with him. He must be one of them. His Galilean accent gives him away."

At this point Peter began to swear he was telling the truth and to invoke a curse on himself if he were lying. "Sir, I don't know what you're saying! I don't know this fellow you're talking about!"

The words were scarcely out of his mouth when immediately the cock crowed a second time. And the Lord turned and looked straight at Peter. Then Peter remembered how he had told him, "Before the cock crows twice tonight you will disown me three times." And he went out and cried bitterly.

Jesus Before the Roman Procurator, Pontius Pilate

As soon as it was morning the chief priests met hurriedly with the elders, the lawyers, and the whole Council and made their plans to get Jesus executed. Then they got up in a body, put Jesus in chains, and led him from the house of Caiaphas to the praetorium to hand him over to Pilate the Governor. They themselves, however, stayed outside the praetorium to avoid defilement so they could celebrate the Passover. It was not yet six o'clock.

Pilate went outside to ask them, "What charge do you bring against this man?"

"We would not have handed him over if he were not a wrongdoer."

"Well, then take him yourselves and try him according to your own law."

"We have no authority to put anybody to death."

Thus they ensured that Jesus' prediction of the kind of death he was going to die would come true. They began to accuse him.

"We caught this man subverting our nation, telling us not to pay taxes to Caesar, and claiming to be the Messiah—a king."

Pilate went back inside the praetorium and summoned Jesus. As Jesus stood before him the Governor asked, "You are the King of the Jews, I take it?"

"Is this your own idea?" Jesus replied. "Or did others suggest it to you?"

"What? Am I a Jew? It's your own nation and their chief priests who have handed you over to me. What have you done?"

"My kingdom does not belong to this world. If it did, my followers would be fighting to keep me from being arrested by the Jews. No, my royal authority has a different origin."

"You are a king then?"

" 'King' is your word. My purpose is to bear witness to the truth. It is for this I was born and for this I have come into the world. And whoever is not deaf to truth hears my voice."

"What is truth?" said Pilate.

He then went back outside and told the chief priests and the mob of Jews, "I cannot find any case against this man."

The chief priests and elders bombarded Jesus with accusations, to which he offered no reply. Pilate turned to him.

"See how many charges they bring against you? Don't you have anything to say in your defense?" But to the Governor's astonishment Jesus did not even answer a word.

They grew even more insistent. "He has been stirring up the people with his teaching throughout Judea. He started in Galilee, and it has spread all the way here."

When Pilate heard this he asked whether the man was a Galilean, and on learning that Jesus belonged to Herod's jurisdiction he turned the case over to him, as Herod himself happened to be in Jerusalem at the time.

Jesus Before Herod Antipas

Herod was very pleased to see Jesus, as he had heard about him and been curious to see him for a long time. He was hoping to see Jesus perform some miracle.

Herod questioned him at length, but Jesus did not answer a word. The chief priests and the lawyers, however, stepped forward and pressed the case against him vigorously.

Finally Herod and his soldiers made fun of Jesus and treated him with contempt, sending him back to Pilate dressed in a gorgeous robe. And that very day Herod and Pilate became friends. There had been a standing feud between them till then.

Pilate Washes His Hands of It All

Pilate now called together the chief priests, councillors, and people.

"You brought this man before me on a charge of subversion. But as you see, I myself have examined him before you and found nothing in him to support the charges. Nor did Herod, since he has referred the case back to us. Clearly this man has done nothing to deserve death. I therefore propose to let him off with a whipping."

But Pilate's words were greeted with a shout. "Do away with him!"

Now at the festival season it was the Governor's custom to set free any one prisoner the crowd asked for. As it happened, there was then in custody a notorious bandit named Jesus Bar-Abbas. He was locked up along with the other rebels who had committed murder in an insurrection that had taken place in the city.

Pilate told the mob, "According to the custom I release one prisoner for you at Passover. Now which one would you like me to release to you—Jesus Bar-Abbas, or Jesus called Messiah, the King of the Jews?"

He knew very well that the chief priests had handed Jesus over because they were jealous. Besides, while he was sitting in judgment his wife sent him a message. "Don't have anything to do with that innocent man. I suffered a lot over him in my dreams last night."

In the meantime the chief priests and the elders stirred up the mob to ask Pilate to set Bar-Abbas free and have Jesus put to death. So when the Governor asked them again, "Which of the two do you want me to release to you?", back came the shout, "Not this man! Give us Bar-Abbas instead!"

Pilate wanted to release Jesus, so he asked them again, "Then what shall I do with Jesus called Messiah, the one you term 'King of the Jews'?"

"Nail him to the cross! Nail him to the cross!" they all screamed.

Pilate spoke to them a third time. "Why? What crime has he committed? I cannot find him guilty of any capital offense. Therefore I shall let him off with a flogging."

With that Pilate took Jesus and had him whipped. The Governor's soldiers brought him inside the praetorium and assembled thc whole company around him. After they had stripped and flogged him they dressed him up in a purple robe. Plaiting a crown from thorns, they put it on his head and a stick in his right hand. They made fun of him, coming up and kneeling in homage, crying, "Hail, King of the Jews!" Then they spat on him, took the stick and beat him over the head, and slapped him around.

Meanwhile the mob outside had been shouting louder and louder, "Nail him to the cross!"

Pilate went out again. "Now look!" he said, "I am bringing him out to *you*, to make you realize *I* don't find any reason to condemn him."

So Jesus came out wearing the crown of thorns and the purple robe.

"Here is the man!" said Pilate.

At the sight of him the chief priests and their henchmen set again to shouting, "Nail him to the cross! Nail him to the cross!"

"You take him," said Pilate, "and crucify him yourselves. For my part I find no reason to condemn him."

The Jews answered back, "We have a law that says he ought to die because he has claimed to be the Son of God."

On hearing this Pilate was very frightened and asked Jesus back inside the praetorium, "Where do you come from?" But Jesus gave him no answer.

"Do you refuse to speak to me? Surely you know I have authority to set you free and likewise to crucify you."

"You would have no authority at all over me if it had not been given you from above. So the one who handed me over to you is guilty of greater sin."

At this point Pilate tried to release him, but the Jews kept shouting, "If you let this man go, you are no friend of Caesar's! Anybody who sets himself up as a king is defying the Emperor!"

Hearing these words, Pilate brought Jesus back outside and took his seat on the tribunal in the spot called the Pavement, and in Hebrew, *Gabbatha.* It was the day of preparation for the Passover, between about eleven o'clock and noon.

"Here is your King!" Pilate called out to the Jews.

"Away with him! Away with him! Nail him to the cross!" they shouted back.

"Must I crucify your King?"

"We have no king but Caesar!" the chief priests replied.

When Pilate saw he was getting nowhere but rather that a riot was brewing he called for some water and washed his hands in full view of the crowd.

"I take no responsibility for the death of this man! This is your doing."

With one voice the people cried, "His blood be on us and on our children!"

So their voice prevailed. Pilate, wishing to appease the mob, passed the sentence they had demanded. He set free the man they wanted—Bar-Abbas—who had been imprisoned for sedition and murder, and handed Jesus over to be crucified.

Judas' Suicide

When Judas the traitor saw Jesus had been sentenced to death he changed his mind and brought back the thirty silver coins to the chief priests and the elders.

"I have sinned," he said, "by betraying an innocent man to his death!"

"What do we care about that? That's your business."

He threw the money down in the Temple and left, and went and hanged himself.

Picking the money up, the chief priests debated what to do with it. "We can't put this in the Temple treasury. It's blood money." So after conferring, they used it to buy the potter's field as a cemetery for foreigners. This explains why that field has been known in their language as *Akeldama* ("Field of Blood") ever since.

Thus Jeremiah's prophecy came true: "They took the thirty silver coins—the price set on his head by the people of Israel—and gave the money for the potter's field, as the Lord directed me."

The Cross

Pilate's soldiers stripped Jesus of the purple, dressed him in his own clothes, and led him out to crucify him, making him carry his own cross. On their way out they met a man from Cyrene—Simon by name, the father of Alexander and Rufus—coming in from the country and pressed him into service to carry Jesus' cross, walking behind him.

Great numbers of people followed. Many women were among them, weeping and wailing for him. Jesus turned to them.

"Do not cry for me, daughters of Jerusalem, but for yourselves and your children. Believe me, the time is coming when people will say, 'How happy the women who were barren, the wombs that never bore a child, the breasts that never nursed one!' Then they will start calling to the mountains, 'Fall on us!' and to the hills, 'Hide us!' If things like this are done when the wood is green, what will happen when it's dried out?"

Two others were with him—criminals being led away to execution. And they came to a spot called the Place of the Skull (in Hebrew, *Golgotha*). There they offered him drugged wine, but after tasting it he refused to drink it. So they nailed him to the cross, likewise nailing the other two to theirs, and set him up in the middle with one bandit on his right hand and the other on his left.

"Father," said Jesus, "forgive them. They don't know what they are doing."

The soldiers took his clothes and divided them in four parts, one for each soldier, except for his tunic. The tunic was seamless, woven all in one piece, so they said to each other, "Let's not tear it. Instead, let's toss to see who gets it."

This happened to make the scripture come true:
"They divided my garments among them,
And gambled for my clothes."
And that is what the soldiers did. After that they sat there and kept watch over him.

Pilate had framed an inscription of the charge against him to be fastened to the cross above his head. It read, "This is Jesus of Nazareth, the King of the Jews." This inscription was read by many of the Jews because the place where Jesus was crucified was not far from the city and the notice was in Hebrew, Latin, and Greek.

The Jewish chief priests complained to Pilate,

"You should not write 'King of the Jews' but rather 'He claimed to be king of the Jews.' "

"What I have written stays written," said Pilate.

The Final Agony

The people stood there watching while passers-by hurled abuse at Jesus, shaking their heads.

"Aha! So you would tear down the Temple, would you, and build it back in three days? Well, why don't you save yourself? Come on down from the cross if you're the Son of God!"

So too the chief priests with the lawyers and elders joked among themselves.

"He saved others. Let him save himself if he is really God's Messiah, his Chosen One. King of Israel indeed! Let him come down from the cross and then we will believe in him. He trusts in God and says he is God's son. Well, let's just see if God wants him enough to rescue him now!"

The soldiers likewise joined in the mockery. They came forward offering him their sour wine. "If you are the King of the Jews, save yourself!"

One of the criminals hanging there with him taunted Jesus. "Aren't you supposed to be the Messiah? Save yourself and us!"

But the other one rebuked him. "Have you no fear of God? We're all under the same sentence. Ours, however, is only just. We are getting what we deserve for what we did. But this man has done nothing wrong." And he said, "Jesus, remember me when you come into your kingdom."

"I tell you this," Jesus answered. "Today you will be with me in Paradise."

Meanwhile near Jesus' cross stood his mother, her sister, Mary the wife of Clopas, and Mary of Magdala.

Jesus saw his mother and the disciple he loved nearby. He said to her, "Woman, there is your son," and to the disciple, "There is your mother." And from that time on the disciple took her to live in his home.

Now from about midday the sun had stopped shining, and it stayed dark over the whole country till about three in the afternoon. At that time Jesus cried out loud.

"*Eli, Eli, lema sabachthani?*" (which means, "My God, my God, why have you deserted me?")

Some of the bystanders on hearing this said, "Listen! He is calling Elijah."

Jesus, aware that everything had now come to its appointed end, said (in fulfillment of scripture), "I am thirsty."

A jar stood there full of sour wine. One of them jumped up, grabbed a sponge and soaked it in the wine, stuck it on a reed, and held it up to Jesus' lips. But the others said, "Wait! Let's see if Elijah will come to save him."

Jesus after taking the wine cried out again. "It is completed!" Then he said, "Father, into your hands I commit my spirit." And with these words he let his head sink down on his chest and breathed his last.

The Temple curtain was ripped in two from top to bottom, and the earth quaked, rocks split apart, and graves gaped open. And many of the saints got up from sleep. Coming out of their graves, they went into the Holy City following his resurrection from the dead, where many people saw them.

When the centurion and his men keeping watch over Jesus saw the earthquake and everything else that happened they were overawed by it all. The centurion, having seen how Jesus died from his position right there in front of the cross, gave praise to God.

"This man was truly a son of God. Beyond all doubt he was innocent."

And all the crowds who had assembled for the spectacle went home beating on their breasts when they saw what had happened.

Jesus' friends had all been standing at a distance watching. A number of women were there, among them Salome, the mother of the sons of Zebedee, Mary of Magdala, and Mary the mother of James the younger and Joseph. These had followed him and furnished assistance when he was in Galilee, and along with them were many other women who had come up to Jerusalem with him.

The Body Taken Down and Buried

Considering that it was the Friday of Passover, the Jews were anxious that the bodies not remain on the crosses on the Sabbath day, since that Sabbath would be an especially solemn one. So they asked Pilate to have the legs broken and the bodies taken down.

The soldiers accordingly came and broke the legs of first one and then the other of the men who had been crucified with Jesus. But when they came to Jesus they found he was already dead, so they did not break his legs. One of the soldiers, however, stabbed his side with a spear, and blood and water flowed out of the wound.

These things happened in fulfillment of the scripture, "Not one of his bones shall be broken." And there is another text that says, "They will look on the one they pierced."

By this time it was getting on towards evening, and it being the day of Preparation (that is, the day before the Sabbath), Joseph of Arimathea made so bold as to seek an audience with Pilate and ask for the body of

Jesus. He was a rich and respected member of the Council, who looked for the coming of God's kingdom. A good and upright man, he had dissented from the Council's decision and action. In fact he was himself a disciple of Jesus, but a secret one for fear of the Jews.

Pilate was surprised to hear that Jesus was already dead and sent for the centurion to ask if Jesus had been dead very long. After receiving the officer's report he gave Joseph permission to take the corpse. So Joseph came to take away the body, accompanied by Nicodemus—the man who had first visited Jesus at night.

Nicodemus brought with him a mixture of myrrh and aloes, more than half a hundredweight, and Joseph had bought a new linen sheet. The two men, taking the body down, wrapped it in the linen with the spices according to the Jews' burial custom.

A garden was there at the place Jesus had been crucified, and in it was a new tomb never yet used for burial, which Joseph had had cut out of the rock for himself. They laid Jesus down in it because it was so close at hand and the Sabbath was almost upon them. And they rolled a big stone against the door of the tomb and left.

The women who had accompanied Jesus from Galilee, including Mary of Magdala and the other Mary, the mother of Joseph, had followed and sat down opposite the grave, taking note of the tomb and how Jesus' body was placed in it. Then they went back to prepare spices and ointments for the body. But they rested throughout the Sabbath in obedience to the commandment.

The next day—the morning after that Friday—the chief priests and the Pharisees came in a group to Pilate.

"Excellency, we recall how that imposter said while

he was still alive, 'I will rise again after three days.' So will you please give orders for the grave to be made secure until the third day, so his disciples won't be able to come and steal the body and then tell the people he was raised from the dead? This last lie would be an even grosser deception than the first!"

"You may take a guard," said Pilate, "and go make the grave as secure as you can."

So they went and made the tomb secure, sealing the stone and leaving the guard on watch.

XI

The Resurrection

The Stone Is Rolled Away

On Saturday evening when the Sabbath was over, the women, including Mary of Magdala, the other Mary, the mother of James, and Salome, bought aromatic oils, intending to go anoint the body of Jesus. That same night they set out to see the tomb.

Suddenly there was a violent earthquake, because one of the Lord's angels came down from heaven, rolled back the stone, and sat down on it. His face shone like lightning and his clothes were white as snow. The guards shook with fear at the sight of him and lay still like dead men.

At early dawn that Sunday morning the women arrived at the tomb bringing the spices they had prepared. They had been wondering, "Who is going to roll the stone away from the door for us?" (It was a big one.) But when they looked up they saw the stone already rolled back. They went inside the tomb, but the body of the Lord Jesus was nowhere to be found.

Mary of Magdala took to her heels and came straight to Simon Peter and the other disciple—the one Jesus loved.

"They have taken the Lord out of the tomb!" she cried. "And we don't know where they have put him!"

While the women were standing in the tomb perplexed, two men in dazzling clothes were suddenly there beside them, one a young man in white sitting on the right side. The women were filled with fear and amazement and bowed their faces to the ground.

"Don't be frightened," the angel told them. "I know you are looking for Jesus of Nazareth who was crucified. But why look for the living among the dead? He is not here. He has risen just as he said. Remember what he told you about the Son of Man while he was still in Galilee—how he must be handed over to the power of sinners, nailed to the cross, and raised to life on the third day?"

They then recalled what he had said.

"Come," the angel continued, "and see the place where they laid him down. Now go quickly and tell his disciples and Peter he has risen from the dead and is preceding you into Galilee. You will see him there as he promised. Now I have told you."

Amazed, they hurried out of the tomb trembling with fear and rapture, and they ran to tell the news to his disciples, too frightened to speak a word to anyone.

Suddenly Jesus was there in their path. As he greeted them they fell prostrate before him, clutching his feet.

"Don't be afraid," Jesus told them. "Go tell my brethren to leave for Galilee. They will see me there."

A Footrace to the Tomb

Peter and the other disciple had dashed out, heading for the tomb. They were both running, but the other disciple outran Peter and reached the tomb first. Stooping over to peek in, he saw the linen wrappings lying there but did not go inside.

Simon Peter came up behind him and went straight into the tomb. He saw the linen wrappings and the cloth that had been around Jesus' head, not lying with them but rolled up in a place by itself. Then the other disciple who had reached the tomb first went in too, and he saw and believed. (They did not yet know the scripture that he must rise from the dead.)

The disciples then went back home.

Jesus Appears to Mary of Magdala

Mary, however, stood crying outside the tomb. As the tears flowed she stooped over to peer into the tomb and saw two angels sitting there where the body of Jesus had been, one at the head and the other at the feet.

"Woman, why are you crying?" they asked her.

"Because they have taken my Lord away, and I don't know where they have put him."

As she spoke she turned around and saw Jesus standing there, but she failed to recognize him.

"Woman, why are you crying?" Jesus asked her. "Who is it you are looking for?"

Thinking he was the gardener, she said, "Sir, if you are the one who removed him, tell me where you have put him, and I will take him away."

"Mary!" he said.

She turned to him and gasped, *"Rabboni!"* (which is Hebrew for "my Teacher").

"Stop holding on to me," he said. "I have not yet gone up to the Father. But go tell my brethren I am going up to my Father and your Father, my God and your God."

Women's Idle Chatter!

Mary of Magdala went to the disciples with her news.

"I have seen the Lord!" she said and gave them his message.

Likewise the other women, Joanna and Mary the mother of James among them, on their return from the tomb reported to the eleven and all the rest, telling their story. But all this impressed the disciples as nonsense. They did not believe them.

The Official Version of What Happened

Meanwhile some of the soldiers guarding the grave had gone back into the city and reported to the chief priests everything that had happened.

After conferring together with the elders the chief priests settled on a plan. They bribed the guards to say, "His disciples came during the night and stole the body while we were asleep." They assured the soldiers, "If this should reach the Governor's ears we'll put matters right with him. We'll see to it you don't have anything to worry about."

So the guards took the money and did as they were told. This is the story that was spread, and it is current among the Jews to this very day.

On the Road to Emmaus

That same day two of the disciples were on their way to a village called Emmaus about seven miles from Jerusalem, and they were talking about all the things that had happened. While they were thus engaged in conversation Jesus himself came up and walked along with them, but something kept their eyes from recognizing him.

"What is this you're debating as you walk?" he asked them.

They halted, their faces full of sadness. Then one of them named Cleopas answered.

"You must be the only visitor in Jerusalem not to know what has been going on there the last few days."

"What things?" asked Jesus.

"The things that have happened to Jesus of Nazareth. This man was a prophet mighty in work and word before God and the whole people. Our chief priests and leaders handed him over to be sentenced to death, and they crucified him. But we had been hoping he was the one to free Israel.

"What's more, this is now the third day since it happened, and some women of our group have come up with a startling tale. They went to the tomb at dawn but failed to find his body. They came back with the story that they had even seen a vision of angels who told them he was alive. Some of our companions went to the grave and found it just as the women had said, but they didn't see any Jesus."

"How foolish you are!" Jesus told them. "How slow to believe everything the prophets have said! Wasn't it necessary for the Messiah to suffer these things and enter his glory?" Then beginning with Moses and all the prophets he explained to them the things regarding him throughout the scriptures.

As they approached the village to which they were going he made as if to go on, but they held him back.

"Stay with us," they urged. "It's getting late, and the day is almost over." So he went in to stay with them.

As they sat down to supper he took the bread and offered thanks to God, then he broke it and gave it to them. Their eyes were opened and they recognized him, but he vanished out of their sight. They turned to each other.

"Didn't we feel our hearts on fire within us while he talked with us on the road and explained the scriptures?"

That selfsame hour they got up and went back to Jerusalem where they found the eleven and their companions all together, saying, "It is true! The Lord has risen! He has appeared to Simon Peter!" The two then recounted what had happened on the road and how they had recognized him when he broke the bread.

Seeing a Ghost?

Now the doors were locked where the disciples were that Sunday evening, because they were afraid of the Jews. But while they were talking about all this, Jesus himself was there standing among them.

"Peace be with you!" he said.

Startled and terrified, they thought they were seeing a ghost.

"Why so perturbed?" he asked. "Why are these doubts cropping up in your minds? Look at my hands and feet. It is I myself. Touch me and see. A ghost doesn't have flesh and bones as you see I have."

After he said this he showed them his hands and his

side. They still could not believe their eyes, but joy began to mix with their wonder.

"Look," he said, "have you anything here to eat?"

They handed him a piece of cooked fish which he took and ate before their very eyes.

"Peace be with you!" Jesus repeated. "These are the very things I told you while I was still with you. Everything written about me in the Law of Moses and in the Prophets and Psalms was bound to come true."

Then he opened their minds to understand the scriptures.

"This is what is written. The Messiah must suffer and on the third day rise from the dead, and in his name repentance and the forgiveness of sins must be proclaimed to all nations beginning from Jerusalem.

"You are the witnesses to these things. Just as the Father sent me, I send you. Look! I bestow on you my Father's promised gift."

So saying, he breathed on them and declared, "Take the Holy Spirit! If you forgive anybody's sins they stand forgiven. If you withhold forgiveness, then unforgiven they remain."

He then led them out as far as Bethany. Raising his hands, he blessed them and in the act of blessing left them. In great joy they returned to Jerusalem and spent all their time in the Temple praising God.

Doubting Thomas

One of the twelve—Thomas called "the Twin"— was not with the rest when Jesus came. So the disciples told him, "We have seen the Lord!"

"Unless I see the nail wounds in his hands," he said, "and put my finger in them and my hand in his side I will not believe!"

A week later the disciples were in the room again, and Thomas was with them. Although the doors were locked, Jesus came and stood among them.

"Peace be with you!" he said. Then he turned to Thomas.

"Put your finger here. See my hands? Now stretch out your hand and put it into my side. Stop your doubting and believe!"

"My Lord and my God!" exclaimed Thomas.

"Do you believe because you have seen me? Happy are those who have not seen yet believe anyway!"

Breakfast by the Sea of Galilee

After this the eleven went to Galilee. Jesus showed himself to the disciples again beside the Sea of Tiberias, and this is how it happened.

Simon Peter and Thomas called "the Twin" were together with Nathanael of Cana-in-Galilee, the sons of Zebedee, and two other disciples. Simon Peter told them, "I'm going fishing."

"We will go with you," they said.

So they went out and launched the boat. But that night they caught nothing.

At daybreak there stood Jesus on the beach. The disciples, however, were unaware that it was Jesus.

"Children, have you caught anything?" he called out.

"No," they shouted back.

"Shoot the net to starboard and you will find some."

They did so and found themselves unable to draw it in, it was so full of fish. The disciple Jesus loved exclaimed to Peter, "It is the Lord!"

When Simon Peter heard that, he knotted his coat around his waist, having stripped for work, and jumped in the sea. The rest came on in the boat towing the net full of fish. They were not far from land, only about a hundred yards.

On coming ashore they saw a charcoal fire there with some fish on it and bread.

"Bring some of your catch," said Jesus.

Simon Peter went aboard and hauled the net to shore. It was full of big fish, a hundred and fifty-three in all. Yet even with so many the net was not torn.

"Come on and have breakfast," Jesus told them.

Now none of the disciples dared ask him, "Who are you?" They knew it was the Lord. Jesus came up, took the bread, and gave it to them and did the same with the fish. This made the third time Jesus appeared to the disciples after he was raised from the dead.

After breakfast Jesus said to Simon Peter, "Simon son of John, do you love me more than these?"

"Yes, Lord, you know I care about you."

"Then feed my lambs."

He asked a second time, "Simon son of John, do you love me?"

"Yes, Lord, you know I care about you."

"Then tend my sheep."

Jesus asked still a third time, "Simon son of John, do you care about me?"

Peter was hurt that he asked him the third time, "Do you care about me?" and responded, "Lord, you know everything. You know I care about you."

"Feed my sheep," said Jesus. "I'm telling you the truth. When you were young you hitched up your belt and went anywhere you pleased, but when you're old you will stretch out your arms and a stranger will tie you fast and carry you where you have no wish to go."

Jesus said this to indicate the kind of death by which Peter was to glorify God. After this he said to Peter, "Follow me."

Peter turned around and saw following them the disciple Jesus loved—the one who had been lying close to Jesus at the supper and had asked the question, "Lord, who is it that's going to betray you?"

When Peter caught sight of him he asked Jesus, "Lord, what about this man?"

"If it should be my will that he stay on till I come, what business is it of yours? Follow me!"

A report thus spread throughout the brotherhood that this disciple would not die. But Jesus did not in fact say he was not to die. He only said, "If it should be my will that he stay on till I come, what business is it of yours?"

On a Mountain in Galilee

The eleven disciples went to the hill in Galilee where Jesus had told them to meet him. He appeared to more than five hundred of the brotherhood at one time, most of whom are still alive though some have died.

When they saw him they fell prostrate before him, though some were doubtful. Coming up, Jesus spoke to them.

"All authority in heaven and on earth has been given me. Go then to all nations and make them my disciples. Baptize them in the name of the Father, the Son, and the Holy Spirit and teach them to observe everything I have commanded you. And rest assured I will be with you always, to the end of the age."

Other Appearances

Jesus then appeared to his brother James and afterwards to all the messengers. Last of all he appeared to Paul too—one, so to speak, born at the wrong time. Over a long period after his death he showed himself to them, speaking about the kingdom of God, and thus giving ample proof that he was alive.

The Ascension From the Mount of Olives

After giving instructions through the Holy Spirit to the messengers he had chosen, Jesus was taken up. While in their company he told them not to leave Jerusalem.

"You must wait for the Father's promise about which you heard me speak. John as you know baptized with water, but before long you will be baptized with the Holy Spirit. So stay here in the city until you are armed with power from above."

While they were all together they asked him, "Lord, is this the time you are going to reestablish the kingdom of Israel?"

"It is not for you to know about dates or times. The setting of these is the Father's own prerogative. Your responsibility is to be witnesses for me in Jerusalem and throughout Judea and Samaria and to the very ends of the earth. And you will be filled with power when the Holy Spirit comes down on you."

When he had said this he was lifted up while they watched, and a cloud took him out of their sight. As they were gazing into the sky at his departure, all of a sudden two men in white stood beside them.

"Galileans," they said, "why stand there looking up at the sky? This Jesus who has been taken away from you to heaven will come back in the same way you have seen him go to heaven."

The disciples then returned to Jerusalem from the Mount of Olives, which is close by, no more than half a mile away. Entering the city, they went to the upstairs room where they were staying—Peter and John and James and Andrew, Philip and Thomas, Bartholomew and Matthew, James the son of Alphaeus and Simon the Zealot, and Judas the son of James. All these joined together in constant prayer with the women, including Mary the mother of Jesus, and with his brothers.

Note on the Composition
of the Book

To make of Jesus' life a narrative as smoothly flowing as a modern novel is impossible without adding purely fictional, imaginary elements to the accounts furnished by the gospel writers. All that they themselves had to work with, as best we can tell from the internal evidence of their books, were oral traditions of important episodes in his life together with collections of his teachings and sayings. The present book adopts this organization by episodes as the only framework for presenting the subject that is faithful to the sources. Titles have been supplied for these episodes and the episodes grouped into chapters to enhance clarity and readability.

The differences in sequence among the various gospel accounts may indicate that even at the time they were written—the last half of the first century A.D.—the actual chronological order of most of these episodes had already passed into oblivion. It is equally conceivable that the gospel writers, unlike the modern historian or biographer, were not particularly concerned with precise chronological order but arranged each his own sequence with an eye to bringing out the significance of the events in the most effective way possible. The order therefore differs among the four simply because their judgment differed. Moreover, many of the teachings and sayings of Jesus may have come down to them with no indication of a setting in time or place, so that each gospel writer had to supply a setting and organization for them himself.

In the composition of this book the sequence the gospel writers themselves derived from or imposed on their materials has been preserved largely intact. The sequence of this book follows generally that of Mark's Gospel. Matthew and Luke have been made to dovetail with that order. The various episodes found only in John's Gospel have been inserted in it at the most appropriate points. Since most scholars agree that Matthew and Luke utilized Mark, Mark's order should probably govern if the sequence is to be dictated at all by the ancient sources.

In inserting the Johannine material the sequence of John's Gospel has also been preserved to the maximum extent. With rare exceptions the order of neither Mark nor John was disturbed unless an episode common to both John and Mark had to be combined to avoid repetition. A good example is Jesus' clearing of the Temple. The combined version of all four gospels' accounts of this event has been placed at the point dictated by Mark rather than at that dictated by John. In contrast, the anointing at Bethany has been placed at the point dictated by John rather than at that dictated by Mark. In both cases the combined episode was placed at the point dictated by whichever of the two furnished the most plausible placement.

The same principles of preserving the sequence already built into the gospels have generally been followed with respect to those portions of Matthew and Luke not found in any other gospel. And combined material common only to Matthew and Luke has been placed at the point dictated by whichever of the two furnished the most plausible placement. Occasionally material found in only one of the two has been put with material on the same subject at the point dictated by the other one. For instance Luke's Parable of the Friend at Midnight is included with the material on prayer in Matthew's Sermon on the Mount. Similarly all apocalyptic references of Jesus have been combined into the segment entitled "Signs of Things to Come" in Chapter IX.

In all cases the order and organization chosen appeared to be the most effective, meaningful, and plausible one possible. No claim is made, however, that this order is necessarily the true order—the order in which the events, sayings, and teachings in fact occurred. It may be, and it may not. The "last word" on this subject is forever beyond our grasp.

In combining variant accounts of the same episode the objective has been to give the fullest account capable of being formed from all the variations to the extent this can be done plausibly. The objective is thus not to reduce any episode to a supposed "original version" or kernel of "historical" fact. Such a quest for the "historical Jesus," even assuming he is other than the one presented us in the New Testament, leads only into a morass of sheer speculation. The objective is rather to present all the information about a particular episode to be gleaned from the entire New Testament to the extent this information is internally compatible.

Episodes have been combined only where they seem clearly to be versions of the same occurrence and where the variations are not great enough to pose any obstacle. On the other hand some episodes, though they may conceivably have been derived from the same historical event, appear in the gospels in two such disparate traditions that any effort to combine them would do violence to both. Good examples are (1) John's account of the healing of the official's boy at Capernaum, and Matthew and Luke's accounts of the healing of the centurion's servant; (2) Nazareth's rejection of Jesus as told by Luke, and the account of the last visit to Nazareth given by Matthew and Mark; and (3) Luke's account of the penitent prostitute who wet Jesus' feet with her tears and wiped them with her hair, and Matthew, Mark, and John's accounts of the dinner at Bethany at which Jesus was anointed.

Two objectives have been paramount in this writing. One has been to avoid repetition as much as possible. Jesus may well have repeated his teachings at different times and places, but there is little point in forcing a modern reader to see virtually the same thing said twice or more times in only slightly different language. Consequently the same teachings, parables, and other sayings have generally been combined. This removal and consolidation was performed, however, only where the matter in question does not appear to have had any substantial connection with the point from which it was removed.

The second objective has been to preserve the contents of all four gospels to the maximum degree. Only where they were found impossible to reconcile was a statement of one of them chosen and that of another one omitted. The choice was made simply on the basis of an assessment of plausibility as influenced by the commentaries of modern scholars. For instance, John says Pilate condemned Jesus to death between eleven o'clock and noon, whereas Mark states that Jesus was crucified between eight and nine o'clock in the morning. Since obviously both cannot be correct, John's statement was adopted and Mark's omitted. Of course Mark may have been right and John wrong, but the reverse seems more likely.

In at least one instance in which John and the synoptic gospels seem incompatible this book adopts a stance in between. John states that the Last Supper took place *before* the Passover and that Jesus was crucified on the afternoon before the evening that was the traditional time for the Passover celebration. Matthew, Mark, and Luke state that the Last Supper *was* the Passover meal. Yet both John and the synoptic tradition agree that the day of the crucifixion was Friday.

This book adopts John's position on the timing of the Last Supper and the crucifixion for the very cogent reason that John at this point purports to be based on the recollections of an eyewitness who was present at the time—"the beloved disciple." Moreover, Mark and Matthew state that the Sanhedrin wanted to get Jesus arrested and executed *before* the Passover—an intention that was thwarted if their timing of the Last Supper and crucifixion be taken as correct. Additionally, a Jewish tradition preserved in the Babylonian Talmud avers that "they hanged Jesus of Nazareth on the Eve of Passover because he practiced sorcery and was leading Israel astray." Finally, what Luke reports was said during the supper seems to make good sense only if the supper was taking place in advance of the usual time for celebration of the Passover.

On the other hand, in John's account of what went on at the supper there are little indications that it *was* a celebration of the Passover. In light of all these data the most plausible solution to the puzzle and the one this book adopts would seem to be that the Last Supper *was* a Passover celebration but that Jesus scheduled it a day ahead of time because he realized the Sanhedrin would try to make its move against him *before* the festival.

Overall there was amazingly little that could not be reconciled. As the Synopsis of the Sources indicates the texts from which each episode or segment of the book is drawn, anyone who wants to compare the combined version with its original sources can do so.

This book is not a fresh translation of the sources from the original Greek. It is simply a retelling of the story in modern American speech. Since the objective is to put that story as nearly as possible into the words Americans would use today, the result may occasionally seem like a rather free paraphrase of the sources, but great care has been taken to make certain that the meaning has not been misrepresented. The reader is invited to compare the book's account of any episode with the source texts as found in any of the widely accepted recent translations of the New Testament.

In this connection it is worth remembering that even in the original New Testament manuscripts we cannot possibly have Jesus' precise words in any event but only their gist or sense. Jesus spoke in the Aramaic language, but the gospels are written in Greek. Even if Jesus had been speaking in Greek, his words would doubtless have reached the gospel writers by the somewhat hazardous process of transmission by word of mouth, because obviously no stenographer was available to take down his words in shorthand.

It must be reemphasized that this book is not a fictionalized account of Jesus' life. Nothing imaginary has been added to the New Testament information. Only what is fairly there has been reproduced here, with one exception. In the account of the imprisonment of John the Baptist an explanation taken from the works of the ancient Jewish historian Flavius Josephus is incorporated, because it is one item of information from a source contemporary with the gospels that is doubtless genuine and throws considerable light on the temper of Israel in Jesus' time.

On the other hand, not everything in the four gospels has been included. Only what they present as historical events of the life of Jesus are presented here. The introductory and concluding remarks of the gospels that do not meet this test are thus omitted.

Likewise commentary by the gospel writers not ascribed to any speaker in the narrative is generally omitted as foreign to the purpose of this book. John 3: 31–36 is a case in point. John 3: 13–21 may be another such instance, but since these latter verses are arguably a continuation of Jesus' discourse to Nicodemus they are included.

The quotations from the Old Testament are always included, however, whether ascribed to a speaker or not, because they obviously have been treated as part and parcel of the story from its very first telling. On the other hand the genealogies of Jesus' ancestors given by

Matthew and Luke are omitted. A table of all such omissions appears in Appendix I under the heading *Portions of the Gospels Omitted as Not Forming Part of the Narrative.*

The other type of omission is of spurious additions to the gospels by ancient copyists that were unknown to the translators of the King James Version but have been uncovered since their time. Although a few of these can perhaps be defended as part of the original manuscripts, it seemed better to disregard all such questionable verses in composing this book. A good example is the ending of the Gospel of Mark, i. e., everything following Mark 16: 8. This ending or, more accurately, *these* endings (they vary in the ancient manuscripts) appear to have been composed by later copyists to make up for what seems to be an otherwise unusually abrupt termination of the book. A table of these omissions appears in Appendix II under the heading *Portions of the Gospels Omitted as Spurious Additions.* Most of these omissions have little significance for a combined narrative such as that presented here, because they usually consist of insertions taken from genuine verses of one of the other gospels. In a combined narrative the omitted matter will show up anyway because it is covered by these genuine verses of another gospel.

One of these "spurious additions" is, however, included in the book, namely John 7: 53 to 8: 11. This episode of the woman caught in adultery has the ring of truth and fits into a combined narrative so perfectly and appropriately that one can hardly doubt it belongs there. In other words, there is little reason to question the genuineness of this piece of tradition. In view of the fact that the four gospels themselves are collections of what were almost certainly at first oral traditions, there seems no reason to exclude this particular episode just because we now know it was not included by the original authors of these collections but by a somewhat later hand. Moreover there is evidence that this tradition was in circulation in the western churches as early as the third or fourth centuries A.D. and one very like it was recounted by Papias as early as the first half of the second century.

It must be remembered that general acceptance among Christians was the test by which the gospels themselves got included in the New Testament rather than the prestige of their supposed authors. Nobody knows for sure who these authors were. The text of none of the four identifies its author by name. Only one—the Gospel of John—identifies its author as an eyewitness of the events, calling him simply "the disciple Jesus loved." Yet as the final chapter of John demonstrates, the gospel in the form in which we have it was not his own work but that of another or a committee of others. And this beloved disciple is stated to be a participant in the events of the narrative starting only from the time of the Last Supper. The ascriptions of the four gospels to Matthew, Mark, Luke, and John respectively are based on church tradition and educated guesses. In the early Church other gospels besides theirs were composed, including one ascribed to Peter and another ascribed to Thomas, but these others failed to win general acceptance and were therefore not included in the Canon.

Apart then from the few verses listed as omitted in the two appendices nothing has been omitted except what little was found to be totally incompatible with the rest.

The disposition of every portion of the New Testament sources utilized can be determined by consulting the Index.

Note on the Historical Setting

Although the point at which Western reckoning of time is divided into B.C. and A.D. is supposed to represent the date of Jesus' birth, he was not in fact born then. Both Matthew and Luke indicate he was born during the reign of Herod the Great, which lasted from at least 37 B.C. until Herod's death in 4 B.C. Jesus must therefore have been born no later than 4 B.C. (The error in our reckoning results from the fact that the person who first devised this system of dating—Dionysius Exiguus in the early sixth century A.D.—picked the wrong Roman year as the dividing point.)

The year in Herod's reign in which Jesus was born cannot be fixed with absolute precision. The only other historical indicator furnished by the gospels is Luke's reference to a census, but which census he meant is uncertain. It is probably the one the Emperor Augustus ordered to be taken of all Roman citizens in 8 B.C. But Luke states that Quirinius was governor of Syria at the time, whereas the governor of Syria in 8 B.C. was in fact C. Sentius Saturninus. Quirinius *was* governor in A.D. 6–7 and is known to have conducted a census in Palestine at that time, but this census is at least ten years too late to have been the one Luke meant. Tertullian writing in the early part of the third century A.D. mentions the nativity census but gives the name of the governor as Saturninus. It is thus likely that the census was that of 8 B.C. and Luke or his source simply made an error over the name of the presiding governor.

A date for Jesus' birth sometime between 8 and 4 B.C. would correspond well with what Matthew tells us about Herod's slaughter of the boys of Bethlehem and its vicinity. There is no corroboration of this particular incident from any source outside Matthew, but Herod is known from other sources to have become almost insanely suspicious of political intrigues against him in the final years of his life. His paranoia, if one may use that term, led him even to execute three of his own fourteen children, two of his sons in 7–6 B.C. and his eldest son only five days before his own death in 4 B.C.

When Jesus' period of activity began and ended and how long it lasted are likewise incapable of precise dating. All four gospels agree it had its inception in the ministry of John the Baptist, and Luke tells us that John the Baptist began to preach in the fifteenth year of the reign of the Emperor Tiberius. By normal Roman reckoning this year ran from August 19, A.D. 28, to August 18, A.D. 29. Jesus would thus have been about thirty-two to thirty-seven years old at this time, assuming a date for his birth around 8 to 4 B.C. If Luke, on the other hand, was using the Jewish method of reckoning the fifteenth year of Tiberius' reign, that year would run from the autumn of A.D. 27 to the autumn of A.D. 28, and Jesus would consequently have been about a year younger. Luke tells us that Jesus was about thirty years old when he began to teach, but John 8:57 may be some indication of an age rather older than thirty.

Since all four gospels agree that Jesus was crucified at Passover by order of Pontius Pilate, the latest date possible for his death was the spring of A.D. 36, because Pilate was removed from the governorship of Judea the following winter. It thus seems reasonably certain that Jesus could not possibly have been older than about forty-three when he was executed. Most scholars guess the year of his death to be sometime around A.D. 29 to 33, perhaps Friday, April 7, A.D. 30. If the latter date be correct, Jesus would have been about thirty-three to thirty-eight years old at the time.

The difficulty in fixing the year of his death stems from the fact that it is impossible to determine from the four gospels how long his period of activity lasted. It may have lasted no more than a year or somewhat longer than three years. Mark, followed by Matthew, seems to indicate a rather short period of activity of great intensity rather than a span of years. These two gospels lead one to believe that Jesus made only one visit to Jerusalem—the Passover pilgrimage that led immediately to his arrest and execution.

The references to various Jewish festivals in John's gospel, on the other hand, may point toward several visits to Jerusalem over a period of at least three years. Some scholars feel these references were intended to have primarily symbolic significance, but even though that is doubtless the case they may also possess chronological significance.

Luke appears at first sight to side with Mark and Matthew against John, but on closer examination this is not so clear. Like Mark and Matthew he recounts only one visit to Jerusalem—the pilgrimage just before Jesus' death—but he locates an enormous amount of his material, namely Luke 9:51 to 19:28, during the course of this pilgrimage. Many of the references in this section of Luke seem difficult to reconcile with such a setting even if the journey were a leisurely one. It is possible that Luke was incorporating in this section traditions of a Judean and Perean ministry that dovetail with the movements of Jesus recorded in John's gospel, and this is the viewpoint adopted in the present book. It seems likely that he developed this section before a copy of Mark came into his hands and then later tried, somewhat less than successfully, to bring it into correspondence with Mark.

This theory gains some support from the fact of a number of concordances between Luke and John in minor details recounted by their gospels. Moreover, the three years mentioned in Luke's Parable of the Barren Fig Tree may conceivably refer to Jesus' own ministry and thereby buttress the apparently three-year period asserted by John's gospel. In other words, for three years Jesus came to Jerusalem looking for fruit on the fig tree—Israel—but found none, so he finally "cut it down" (as Mark and Matthew almost literally say he did to an actual tree near Jerusalem during the last week of his life). Luke 23:5 may also indicate a rather extensive ministry in Judea in contrast with Mark and Matthew.

It is impossible in this brief space to outline the entire previous history of the Jewish people, collectively known as Israel. Suffice it to say that the Jews of Jesus' time looked back to their golden age under their kings David and Solomon about ten centuries earlier. The Hebrew state that had been consolidated by David and Solomon had later split into two separate kingdoms—a northern kingdom called Israel and a southern one called Judah. The northern kingdom was overrun and obliterated by the Assyrians about 722 B.C. The southern one was conquered by the Babylonians about 586 B.C., and many of its people were carried off into captivity in Babylon. When Babylon fell prey itself to the advancing Persian Empire about 539 B.C. the Persian king Cyrus allowed the exiles to return to Palestine where they rejoined their compatriots in Judah and rebuilt the Temple at Jerusalem.

The Jews remained subjects of the Persian Empire until it was conquered by Alexander the Great of Macedon. From his death in 323 B.C. until long after the time of Jesus Greek language and culture permeated the entire Near East. Even many Jews became Hellenized.

Since Alexander had not groomed anyone to succeed him, his generals proceeded to fight over his empire. One of them—Ptolemy—managed to secure Egypt, and another—Seleucus—gained Syria. For many years Palestine was a pawn in the territorial struggles between their two dynasties. The Seleucid dynasty finally won control of it about 198 B.C.

Greek manners, morals, language, and religion might well have swallowed up the Jews completely but for the stupidity of one of these Greek kings of Syria who succeeded Seleucus. This king—Antiochus IV Epiphanes—decided to Hellenize the Jews forcibly by prohibiting further observance of their religious practices and substituting pagan worship instead. His desecration of the Temple in 168 B.C. is what the prophet Daniel refers to as the "abomination of desolation."

His action galvanized the Jews into open rebellion. Under the leadership of the Maccabees the revolt succeeded and by 142 B.C. had managed to achieve virtual independence for Israel. The rededication of the Temple by the Maccabees is still celebrated in the Jewish festival of Hanukkah. Unfortunately the successors of the Maccabees fell to squabbling and fighting among themselves, and one of them finally appealed to the Romans for help. The latter were only too glad to oblige. In 63 B.C. a Roman army under Pompey occupied Palestine, and Israel fell under the dominion of Rome.

During their brief period of independence, however, the Jews had expanded their territory by conquest, imposing their religion on the conquered peoples. Among these were the people of Galilee and an Idumean ruler by the name of Antipater. This Idumean who had been forced to adopt Judaism was eventually appointed by the Romans to govern Judea and was the father of Herod the Great. Thus Herod was only nominally a Jew, and in fact his outlook was completely pagan.

In 40 B.C. during an invasion by the Parthians Herod fled to Rome where, with the help of Mark Antony and Octavian (who later became the Emperor Augustus), he gained recognition from the Roman Senate as king of the Jews and acquired military help to retake the invaded territory. The meager extent of his attachment to the Jewish religion can be seen in the fact that he offered a sacrifice to Jupiter for this good fortune.

Herod sought to buttress his legitimacy in Jewish

eyes by taking as his second wife the Maccabean princess Mariamne and curried favor with his Jewish subjects by rebuilding the Temple at Jerusalem on a magnificent scale, but he never became a popular ruler. He himself was responsible for Mariamne's death, and as already noted, his two sons by her were put to death in the closing years of his reign.

The Roman Empire had been inaugurated in 27 B.C., not many years before Jesus' birth. Jesus was thus born in the reign of the first emperor—Augustus—and put to death in the reign of his immediate successor Tiberius. At that time Rome's dominion already extended from the English Channel to Arabia and almost completely encircled the Mediterranean Sea, imposing a peace throughout this vast region that made not only for a great expansion of trade and commerce but also for the widest dissemination of ideas and culture. But not all parts of the Empire were under direct Roman administration. Some parts the Romans permitted to be governed by puppet kings and princes. One such part was Palestine, where political authority was wielded by this puppet king Herod the Great.

For the most part the law applied in Palestine as elsewhere was the local traditional law of the subject people rather than Roman law. The Roman overlords were principally interested in keeping the peace, suppressing insurrection, and collecting taxes. They were otherwise generally tolerant of local religious customs and traditions that differed from their own. The collection of taxes they farmed out to natives of the region. These tax collectors or "publicans" were held in hatred and contempt by the local populace not only for their collaboration with the alien power and the odiousness of their exactions but also because the people had no way of knowing just how much was due. Thus the tax collectors were able to, and did, feather their own nests at the people's expense. Indeed they were expected to do so.

Several regions of Palestine figure prominently in Jesus' life:

(1) Judea proper in the south, situated between the Mediterranean Sea on the west and the Dead Sea and the lower stretches of the Jordan River on the east. Jerusalem and the towns of Bethlehem, Bethphage, Bethany, Emmaus, Ephraim, Jericho, and Arimathea were all located here. The appellation "Jews" was often used to refer to inhabitants of this region. The area just south of Judea was known as Idumea.

(2) Galilee in the north, extending westward toward the Phoenician coast from the shore of the large fresh-water lake (variously called Sea of Galilee, Sea of Tiberias, and Lake of Gennesaret) from which the Jordan River flows south to the Dead Sea. Capernaum, Chorazin, and Magdala were on the plain probably called Gennesaret which is situated along the western shore of the lake, while Nazareth, Cana, and Nain were farther southwest in the hilly interior of the region.

(3) Samaria, sandwiched between Galilee to the north and Judea to the south. Samaria was occupied by a polyglot people partly of Jewish ancestry whose religion was basically derived from Judaism. The Jews, however, despised them as aliens and heretics and were equally despised in return. This mutual hostility was so great that Jews making the pilgrimage from Galilee to Jerusalem for the religious festivals would often take the roundabout way down the Jordan River valley on the eastern border of Samaria in order to avoid having to pass through it.

(4) Phoenicia, along the coast of the Mediter-

ranean Sea to the west and north of Galilee. The cities of Tyre and Sidon were located on this coast of what is now modern Lebanon.

(5) Iturea and Trachonitis, situated northeast of the Sea of Galilee. The capital of this region, called Philip's Caesarea to distinguish it from the Caesarea built by Herod the Great on the coast of Samaria, was located almost due north of the Sea of Galilee, and Mt. Hermon—the mountain probably meant by the gospel writers as the site of the Transfiguration—was just beyond. Bethsaida on the shore of the Sea of Galilee was situated in this jurisdiction.

(6) The Ten Towns ("Decapolis"), spreading east and southeast from the shores of the Sea of Galilee. This was a largely Gentile territory comprised of ten semi-autonomous municipalities. The episode of the Gerasene Madman took place on this eastern shore of the lake, and probably also the Feeding of the Four Thousand, who may well have been Gentiles. This explains the presence of herds of pigs—animals whose meat was anathema to Jews.

(7) Perea, the region flanking Judea and Samaria on the eastern or "far side" of the Jordan River and Dead Sea. Herod Antipas imprisoned John the Baptist in his fortress of Macherus here.

These regions were generally within the confines of the larger territory known as Syria, which also extended beyond them to the north and east. The Gentile woman at Tyre whose daughter Jesus healed was thus called a "Phoenician Syrian." This is doubtless also the reason why Luke referred to the governor of Syria in identifying the nativity census.

It should not be supposed that Palestine was a backwater of the Empire. It lay then as now right at the crossroads of the overland routes linking Europe with Egypt and the rest of Africa on the one hand, and with Mesopotamia, Persia, India, and the rest of Asia on the other. In view of its position athwart these important trade routes, foreigners passing through must have been a common sight and Greek must have been widely known and used as the common language of trade and commerce and of government as well. From the direct quotations of Jesus found in Mark particularly, it is apparent that Jesus' mother tongue was Aramaic—a Semitic language very closely akin to ancient classical Hebrew—but educated Jews also knew Hebrew because most of their religious books, including "the Law and the Prophets," were written in it.

The Romans had adopted Greek culture almost lock, stock, and barrel, and many Romans knew and spoke Greek in addition to, or instead of, Latin. The New Testament documents came to be written in the common Greek idiom, called *Koiné* to distinguish it from ancient classical Greek. This ordinary Greek speech was generally the means of communication between persons who did not share the same native language, at least throughout the eastern part of the Empire.

Unlike the Greeks and Romans who had many gods the Jews were monotheistic. The name they gave the one God they worshipped—*Yahweh* (of which "Jehovah" is a corruption)—means simply "I am." In John's gospel these words "I am" are often found on the lips of Jesus, sometimes without any predicate.

There was no division between church and state in ancient Jewish polity and no distinction between law and morality. Though King Herod exercised political authority, the law as well as the ethics of the Jews was the Law of Moses—the "Pentateuch" or first five books of the Old Testament. And national life centered around the Temple at Jerusalem just as local life in the provincial towns centered around the synagogue.

At the apex of this theocracy was the Sanhedrin—the national council made up of the elders of the people, the chief priests, and the recognized interpreters of the Law who in the gospels are called either "scribes" or "lawyers." The term "lawyers" has been utilized throughout the present book in preference to "scribes," though these people were not hired advocates in the sense of lawyers today.

The Jews of Jesus' time were by no means confined to Palestine. There were large numbers of them in far-flung settlements in almost every corner of the known world—in Mesopotamia, in northern Syria and the coastal cities of Asia Minor, in the Greek islands, in Alexandria, Egypt, and even in Rome itself. All these Jews of "the Dispersion" looked to Jerusalem as their metropolis, but many of them had ceased to understand Hebrew and knew only Greek. The Law of Moses was deemed binding on every Jew at all times, whether he was a resident of the homeland or dispersed abroad and wherever he happened to be at the moment. So the Old Testament came to be translated into Greek in the two centuries or so before Jesus. This Greek version, called the *Septuagint,* provided the gospel writers with many of their quotations of scripture (which are not always accurate renditions of the original Hebrew).

The difficulty of observing the Law of Moses in all its minute details led those who were seriously determined to do so to organize themselves into brotherhoods for mutual support and instruction. These "brethren" had come to be known by the time of Jesus as "Pharisees"—a word that may have meant "the separated ones." They doubtless considered themselves, and other people regarded them, as separate from the rabble "who care nothing for the Law." They were respected and influential, especially in the local synagogues. John 1:26 may mean that Jesus himself was originally a member of one of these brotherhoods. If that is the case he would have been quite familiar with their ways of thinking.

Another group mentioned in the gospels, however, constituted the real Jewish "Establishment" in the Palestine of the time, in the sense in which that word is used today. These were the Sadducees. Heirs of the Maccabean war of independence against Syria, they were mainly comprised of the land-owning aristocracy and the chief priests and probably dominated the Sanhedrin. They were primarily concerned with maintaining the Jewish theocratic state as a distinct entity in the homeland—an objective that plainly compelled them to avoid direct confrontation with the might of Rome. They differed from the Pharisees on many burning issues of the time. For instance they rejected the Pharisaic acceptance of oral and written tradition and customs outside the Pentateuch as authoritative, viewing many of these as alien importations from Persian and Greek culture.

In Judea the Sanhedrin—presided over by the High Priest—exercised substantial authority within limits set by the imperial authorities. Because of the presence of the Temple in Jerusalem the priestly hierarchy held overriding influence and prestige there. The office of High Priest was hereditary in certain families and was held by Annas from A.D. 6 to A.D. 15 when he was induced or forced to retire. His son-in-law Caiaphas was High Priest during Jesus' period of activity, but Annas remained the power behind the throne so to speak. This is probably why the gospels call this period "the high-priesthood of Annas and Caiaphas" though in fact there was only one High Priest in office at any given time.

The more volatile elements of Palestinian Jewry stood outside the Establishment. Various sects had their own peculiar doctrines and practices. Some of these—such as the Qumran sect which left us the Dead Sea Scrolls—had retired into isolated communities by themselves to practice their own fanatical brand of piety. Undoubtedly many of these were ferociously nationalistic and looked forward to a war of liberation in which the Jews would drive the hated Romans from their soil.

Although Rome ruled with an iron hand everywhere, most of the subject peoples of the Empire were content with Roman government because it was at least an improvement over the constant wars, anarchy, and misrule of previous eras. But not the Jews. They never forgot their brief and glorious spell of independence under the Maccabees and never lost their determination to regain it. Citing prophecies found in the Old Testament and in some of the Jewish intertestamental literature, they looked forward to the coming of a great prophet—the Messiah—who would be the anointed king of Israel just like their kings of old. This glorious figure called "the Son of David" would reestablish the throne of his royal ancestor and restore Israel to a new golden age like the one it had enjoyed under David and Solomon.

The more fanatical actually participated in an underground resistance movement against the Romans which broke out in sporadic insurrections. They called themselves Zealots ("patriots"), but the Romans called them "bandits" and dealt with them, whenever they could catch them, by the slow and cruel means of execution known as crucifixion. Dying men hanging on crosses served as prominent and grisly reminders of the consequences of rebellion to the rest of the populace. Many of these so-called "bandits" made their hideouts in the rocks and caves of the Judean desert just west of the Jordan River and preyed on passing travelers and caravans. We today would have called them guerrillas.

The Zealots found plenty of sympathizers among the people, especially in Galilee, which was a hotbed of Jewish disaffection and unrest. Although many of the Galileans who regarded themselves as Jews were descended from non-Jews forcibly "converted" when the Maccabean state conquered their territory, they outdid the Judeans in their religious and nationalistic fervor. In A.D. 6 when Jesus was not much more than ten years old a certain Judas of Galilee had led an abortive uprising against the Romans. It is therefore hardly surprising that Josephus and the gospels say Herod Antipas was afraid of the people and clapped John the Baptist in prison to forestall a potential rebellion. The imperial authorities in Judea kept on continual alert whenever the Galileans descended in thousands on Jerusalem at the Jewish religious festivals. At such times Pilate was accustomed to leave his seat of government at the coastal port of Caesarea (the one built by Herod the Great) and take up residence in the praetorium at Jerusalem with a sizeable force of troops. Apparently one such insurrection broke out at the fateful Passover at which Jesus himself was arrested, because all four gospels agree that he was crucified along with two of these so-called "bandits," while a third one—Bar-Abbas (which means "son of the father")—was released.

Into this ferment of anticipation about the coming of the Messiah Jesus was born. In A.D. 66, some thirty-odd years after his death, the full-scale rebellion finally flared. The Romans did not succeed in retaking Jerusalem until A.D. 70 when Titus' legions captured it and destroyed the Temple. Even then a few pockets of resistance held out longer, such as the gallant force at Masada that eventually committed suicide rather than surrender. Titus' triumph is commemorated by a great arch at Rome that can still be seen resplendent with friezes of Jewish candelabra and Temple vessels. Still another full-scale revolt occurred in A.D. 132, and this time the Romans determined to put an end to such threats once and for all. The rebels were mercilessly slaughtered and the province of Judea was wiped off the map of the Empire.

It is one of the bitter ironies of history that Jesus was rejected by many of his fellow Jews because he firmly resisted their attempts to make him into, and to define him in terms of, their own notion of the role of the "Son of David," yet their leaders eventually got him executed like any common bandit for that very same role he had resolutely declined.

Besides this current of Messianic hope there was also prevalent in the Jewish religious life of the day a powerful strain of apocalyptic vision. This was very much in evidence in the Qumran sect. It involved a firm conviction that time was drawing to a close and the final cosmic struggle between good and evil was at hand. Evil was personified by the belief in devils, and many people considered madness and disease to be the result of demon possession and of sin. The coming of the Messiah was bound up with this notion of the end of the age.

Shortly after Jesus' birth Herod the Great died. His will, which he had changed a number of times, divided his realm, naming his son Herod Archelaus king of Judea, Samaria, and Idumea. It was, however, subject to confirmation by the Emperor. Archelaus went to Rome to get Augustus to appoint him king, but a deputation of Jews went too in order to try to block the appointment. This actual event of history is woven as a subplot into Luke's version of the Parable of the Money in Trust.

Augustus finally decided to confirm the division of Herod's realm. He assigned Judea, Samaria, and Idumea to Archelaus but gave him the title of ethnarch instead of king. Galilee and Perea he assigned to Archelaus' brother Herod Antipas, and Iturea and Trachonitis to their half-brother Philip, granting these latter two the lesser title of tetrarch.

This Philip was another son of Herod the Great by a different wife and was not the one that Herodias left in order to marry Herod Antipas. The latter person—Herodias' former husband—was a half-brother of the others, a son of Herod the Great by still another wife. Herodias herself was the daughter of another one of the sons of Herod the Great, namely Aristobulus, who was one of Herod's sons by Mariamne.

The dynasty founded by Herod the Great did have its supporters among the people. These supporters are called "Herodians" in the gospels. Philip managed successfully to govern his territory until his death in A.D. 34. Herod Antipas ruled Galilee and Perea until A.D. 39 when he was deposed by the Emperor Caligula—

Tiberius' successor—for conspiracy. He was banished to Gaul (modern France). Archelaus, however, achieved such a reputation for cruelty within ten years of his accession that Augustus deposed him in A.D. 6 and placed Judea and Samaria under direct Roman administration. A Roman official of secondary rank called a "perfect" and later a "procurator" was made governor of this newly organized Roman province. One of these—a soldier by the name of Pontius Pilate—was ruling Judea and Samaria from A.D. 26 to 37, during the period of Jesus' activity. He was also removed from office after the massacre of a group of Samaritans engaged in an innocent religious mission. Only after Jesus' death was the entire realm of Herod the Great reunited under a single ruler. This was Herod Agrippa I, who was a grandson of Herod the Great. He was the brother of Herodias. But it remained united for only a very brief period (A.D. 41–44).

The presence in Palestine of so many jurisdictions under separate governance made it easy for Jesus to avoid arrest and thereby to pick and choose his own good time. The Sea of Galilee in particular, bordering three of them—Galilee on the western shore, Iturea and Trachonitis on the northern, and the Ten Towns on the eastern—was an almost ideal site for the teaching of such a controversial individual. If threatened with arrest on the Galilean side of the lake he could simply board a boat and cross to one of the other territories beyond the reach of the Galilean authorities.

Such in brief is the setting of the events the New Testament gospels unfold.

Synopsis of the Sources

9. John Imprisoned by Herod Antipas
    Matt. 4: 12
    Mark 1: 14
    Luke 3: 19–20. 4:14
    John 4: 1–4
    Josephus, *Antiquities of the Jews,* Bk. XVIII, ch. V, 2

10. The Samaritan Woman
    John 4: 5–43

III. THE "GALILEAN SPRINGTIME"

1. Jesus Arrives in Galilee
    Matt. 4: 17
    Mark 1: 14–15
    Luke 4: 14–15
    John 4: 45

2. The Official's Boy
    John 4: 46–54

3. Nazareth Rejects Jesus
    Luke 4: 16–30

4. Jesus Calls Four Fishermen to Follow Him
    Matt. 4: 13–16, 18–22
    Mark 1: 16–20
    Luke 4: 31. 5: 1–11

5. "Even the Demons Obey Him"
    Mark 1: 21–28
    Luke 4: 31–37

6. Peter's Mother-in-Law
    Matt. 8: 14–17. 4: 23–25
    Mark 1: 29–39
    Luke 4: 38–44

7. Jesus Touches the Untouchable
    Matt. 8: 2–4
    Mark 1: 40–45
    Luke 5: 12–16

39. The Gerasene Madman
    Matt. 8: 28–34
    Mark 5: 1–20
    Luke 8: 26–39

40. Jairus' Daughter and the Woman With the Hemorrhage
    Matt. 9: 18–26
    Mark 5: 21–43
    Luke 8: 40–56

41. The Blind See and the Dumb Speak
    Matt. 9: 27–34

42. The Last Visit to Nazareth
    Matt. 13: 54–58
    Mark 6: 1–6
    John 4: 44

43. The Mission of the Twelve
    Matt. 9: 35–38. 10: 1, 5–16, 24–33, 37–42. 11: 1
    Mark 6: 6–13. 9: 41
    Luke 9: 1–6. 12: 4–9. 17: 33
    John 13: 20

44. John Is Beheaded
    Matt. 14: 1–12
    Mark 6: 14–29
    Luke 9: 7–9

IV. THE TRAINING OF THE TWELVE IN AND AROUND GALILEE

1. The Feeding of the Five Thousand
   Matt. 14: 13–21
   Mark 6: 30–44
   Luke 9: 10–17
   John 6: 1–13

2. Jesus Comes to His Disciples Across Stormy Waters
   Matt. 14: 22–36
   Mark 6: 45–56
   John 6: 14–21

3. "I Am the Real Bread"
   John 6: 22–71. 7: 1

4. What Defiles a Person?
   Matt. 15: 1–20
   Mark 7: 1–15, 17–23
   Luke 11: 37–38. 6: 39–40

5. The Gentile Woman's Daughter
   Matt. 15: 21–28
   Mark 7: 24–30

6. The Deaf Mute
   Mark 7: 31–37

7. The Feeding of the Four Thousand
   Matt. 15: 29–39
   Mark 8: 1–10

8. "Beware of the Yeast of the Pharisees and Sadducees"
   Matt. 16: 1, 4–12
   Mark 8: 11–21

9. The Blind Man of Bethsaida
   Mark 8: 22–26

10. "Who Do You Say I Am?"*
    Matt. 16: 13–28
    Mark 8: 27–38. 9: 1
    Luke 9: 18–27

11. The Transfiguration
    Matt. 17: 1–13
    Mark 9: 2–13
    Luke 9: 28–36. 17: 25

12. The Epileptic Boy
    Matt. 17: 14–19
    Mark 9: 14–29
    Luke 9: 37–43

13. Faith Like a Mustard Seed
    Matt. 17: 20
    Luke 17: 5–6

14. Jesus Again Predicts His Death
    Matt. 17: 22–23
    Mark 9: 30–32
    Luke 9: 43–45

15. The Temple Tax
    Matt. 17: 24–27

16. "Who Will Be Greatest in God's Kingdom?"
    Matt. 18: 1–4
    Mark 9: 33–36, 49–50
    Luke 9: 46–48

17. "Guard Yourselves and the Children from Temptation"
    Matt. 18: 5–10, 14. 5: 29–30
    Mark 9: 37, 42–43, 45, 47–48
    Luke 9: 48. 17: 1–3

18. "If He's Not Against Us, He's For Us"
    Mark 9: 38–40
    Luke 9: 49–50

19. "When a Brother Does Wrong"
    Matt. 18: 15–20

20. "Forgiveness Must Be Unlimited"
    Matt. 18: 21–22
    Luke 17: 3–4

21. The Parable of the Merciless Servant
    Matt. 18: 23–35

22. Jesus Decides to Go to Jerusalem
    Luke 9: 51–56
    John 7: 2–10

V. IN JERUSALEM AND JUDEA

1. Jesus at the Festival of Tabernacles
    John 7: 11–52. 8: 12–59

2. The Man Born Blind
    John 9: 1–41

13. The Parable of the Money in Trust
    Matt. 25: 14–30
    Luke 19: 11–28

VIII. JERUSALEM! JERUSALEM!

  1. Anointed as King, But in Order to Die
     Matt. 26: 6–13
     Mark 14: 3–9
     John 11: 55–57. 12: 1–11

  2. The Triumphal Entry
     Matt. 21: 1–11, 14–17
     Mark 11: 1–11
     Luke 19: 29–44
     John 12: 12–19

  3. The Barren Fig Tree: The Parable Acted Out
     Matt. 21: 18–19
     Mark 11: 12–14

  4. The Clearing of the Temple
     Matt. 21: 12–13
     Mark 11: 15–18
     Luke 19: 45–46, 47–48
     John 2: 14–22

  5. Faith to Move Mountains
     Matt. 21: 19–22
     Mark 11: 19–25
     Luke 19: 47. 21: 37–38
     John 7: 53. 8: 1

  6. The Woman Caught in Adultery
     John 8: 2–11

  7. The Sanhedrin Challenges Jesus' Authority
     Matt. 21: 23–27
     Mark 11: 27–33
     Luke 20: 1–8

  8. The Parable of the Two Sons
     Matt. 21: 28–32

IX. JESUS PREPARES HIS DISCIPLES FOR HIS DEATH

1. Signs of Things to Come
   Matt. 24: 1–41. 10: 17–23
   Mark 13: 1–32
   Luke 21: 5–33. 12: 11–12. 17: 31–32, 22–24, 37, 26–30, 34–35

2. "So Be Prepared!"
   Matt. 24: 42
   Mark 13: 33–36
   Luke 21: 34–36. 12: 35–38

3. The Parables of the Burglar and the Servant in Charge
   Matt. 24: 43–51
   Mark 13: 37
   Luke 12: 39–48

4. The Parable of the Ten Bridesmaids
   Matt. 25: 1–13

5. The Last Judgment
   Matt. 25: 31–46

6. Jesus Predicts His Crucifixion
   Matt. 26: 1–5
   Mark 14: 1–2
   Luke 22: 1–2

7. Thirty Silver Coins
   Matt. 26: 14–16
   Mark 14: 10–11
   Luke 22: 3–6

8. The Preparations for the Passover
   Matt. 26: 17–19
   Mark 14: 12–16
   Luke 22: 7–13

9. Jesus Arrives With the Twelve
   Matt. 26: 20
   Mark 14: 17
   Luke 22: 14–16, 24–26, 28–30

10. Jesus Washes His Disciples' Feet
    Luke 22: 27
    John 13: 1–19

11. Jesus Points Out His Betrayer
    Matt. 26: 21–25
    Mark 14: 18–21
    Luke 22: 21–23
    John 13: 21–30

12. The Memorial of the Last Supper
    Matt. 26: 26–29
    Mark 14: 22–25
    Luke 22: 17–19
    1 Cor. 11: 23–25

13. "Before the Cock Crows, You Will Disown Me"
    Matt. 26: 31–35
    Mark 14: 27–31
    Luke 22: 31–38
    John 13: 31–38

14. Jesus' Farewell to His Disciples
    John 14. 15. 16

15. Jesus Prays for His Disciples
    John 17

16. In the Garden of Gethsemane
    Matt. 26: 30, 36–46
    Mark 14: 26, 32–42
    Luke 22: 39–46
    John 18: 1–2

X. THE ARREST, TRIAL, CRUCIFIXION, AND BURIAL

1. The Kiss of Judas
    Matt. 26: 47–56
    Mark 14: 43–52
    Luke 22: 47–54
    John 18: 3–12

2. An Informal Interrogation
   John 18: 12–14, 19–24

3. The Examination Before the Sanhedrin
   Matt. 26: 57, 59–68
   Mark 14: 53, 55–65
   Luke 22: 54, 63–71

4. Peter's Denial
   Matt. 26: 58, 69–75
   Mark 14: 54, 66–72
   Luke 22: 54–61
   John 18: 15–18, 25–27

5. Jesus Before the Roman Procurator, Pontius Pilate
   Matt. 27: 1–2, 11–14
   Mark 15: 1–5
   Luke 23: 1–7
   John 18: 28–38

6. Jesus Before Herod Antipas
   Luke 23: 8–12

7. Pilate Washes His Hands of It All
   Matt. 27: 15–30
   Mark 15: 6–19
   Luke 23: 13–16, 18–25
   John 18: 39–40. 19: 1–16

8. Judas' Suicide
   Matt. 27: 3–10
   Acts 1: 16–19

9. The Cross
   Matt. 27: 31–38
   Mark 15: 20–27
   Luke 23: 26–34, 38
   John 19: 16–25

10. The Final Agony
    Matt. 27: 39–56
    Mark 15: 29–41
    Luke 23: 35–37, 39–49

John 19: 25–30
1 Cor. 15: 3

11. The Body Taken Down and Buried
Matt. 27: 57–66
Mark 15: 42–47
Luke 23: 50–56
John 19: 31–34, 36–42
1 Cor. 15: 4

XI. THE RESURRECTION

1. The Stone Is Rolled Away
Matt. 28: 1–10
Mark 16: 1–8
Luke 24: 1–8
John 20: 1–2
1 Cor. 15: 4

2. A Footrace to the Tomb
John 20: 3–10

3. Jesus Appears to Mary of Magdala
John 20: 11–17

4. Women's Idle Chatter!
Luke 24: 9–11
John 20: 18

5. The Official Version of What Happened
Matt. 28: 11–15

6. On the Road to Emmaus
Luke 24: 13–35
1 Cor. 15: 5

7. Seeing a Ghost?
Luke 24: 36–39, 41–49, 50–53
John 20: 19–23
1 Cor. 15: 5

8. Doubting Thomas
John 20: 24–29
1 Cor. 15: 5

9. Breakfast by the Sea of Galilee
   Matt. 28: 16
   John 21: 1–23

10. On a Mountain in Galilee
    Matt. 28: 16–20
    1 Cor. 15: 6

11. Other Appearances
    Acts 1: 3
    1 Cor. 15: 7–8

12. The Ascension From the Mount of Olives
    Luke 24: 49
    Acts 1: 2, 4–14

Appendix I

**Portions of the Gospels Omitted as
Not Forming Part of the Narrative**

Matt. 1: 1–17

Mark 1: 1

Luke 1: 1–4
Luke 3: 23–38

John 1: 1–5, 7–14, 16–18
John 3: 31–36
John 19: 35
John 20: 30–31
John 21: 24–25

Appendix II

Portions of the Gospels Omitted as Spurious Additions

Matt. 16: 2–3

Matt. 17: 21

Matt. 18: 11

Matt. 21: 44

Matt. 23: 14

Mark 7: 16

Mark 9: 44, 46

Mark 11: 26

Mark 15: 28

Mark 16: 9–20

Luke 17: 36

Luke 22: 19–20, 62

Luke 23: 17

Luke 24: 12, 40

John 5: 3–4

Index

This index is provided to enable the reader to ascertain the disposition of every verse of the sources. Apart from page numbers, there are references to the Appendixes which contain lists of omitted texts.

267